DATA GOVERNAN

BCS, THE CHARTERED INSTITUTE FOR IT

BCS, The Chartered Institute for IT, is committed to making IT good for society. We use the power of our network to bring about positive, tangible change. We champion the global IT profession and the interests of individuals, engaged in that profession, for the benefit of all.

Exchanging IT expertise and knowledge
The Institute fosters links between experts from industry, academia and business to promote new thinking, education and knowledge sharing.

Supporting practitioners
Through continuing professional development and a series of respected IT qualifications, the Institute seeks to promote professional practice tuned to the demands of business. It provides practical support and information services to its members and volunteer communities around the world.

Setting standards and frameworks
The Institute collaborates with government, industry and relevant bodies to establish good working practices, codes of conduct, skills frameworks and common standards. It also offers a range of consultancy services to employers to help them adopt best practice.

Become a member
Over 70,000 people including students, teachers, professionals and practitioners enjoy the benefits of BCS membership. These include access to an international community, invitations to a roster of local and national events, career development tools and a quarterly thought-leadership magazine. Visit www.bcs.org/membership to find out more.

Further information
BCS, The Chartered Institute for IT,
3 Newbridge Square,
Swindon, SN1 1BY, United Kingdom.
T +44 (0) 1793 417 417
(Monday to Friday, 09:00 to 17:00 UK time)
www.bcs.org/contact
http://shop.bcs.org/

DATA GOVERNANCE
Governing data for sustainable business

Edited by Alison Holt

bcs
The
Chartered
Institute
for IT

The right of Alison Holt, Benoit Aubert, Geoff Clarke, Frédéric Gelissen, Abdelaziz Khadraoui, Rohan Light, Nathalie de Marcellis-Warin, Alisdair Mckenzie, Li Ming, Rose Pan, Beenish Saeed and David Sutton to be identified as authors and editors of this work has been asserted by them in accordance with sections 77 and 78 of the Copyright, Designs and Patents Act 1988.

Published by BCS Learning and Development Ltd, a wholly owned subsidiary of BCS, The Chartered Institute for IT, 3 Newbridge Square, Swindon, SN1 1BY, UK.
www.bcs.org

Paperback ISBN: 978-1-78017-3757
PDF ISBN: 978-1-78017-3764
ePUB ISBN: 978-1-78017-3771
Kindle ISBN: 978-1-78017-3788

Ebook available

British Cataloguing in Publication Data.
A CIP catalogue record for this book is available at the British Library.

Publisher's acknowledgements
Reviewers: Nigel Turner and Ian Wallis
Publisher: Ian Borthwick
Commissioning editor: Rebecca Youé
Production manager: Florence Leroy
Project manager: Sunrise Setting Ltd
Copy-editor: The Business Blend Ltd
Proofreader: Barbara Eastman
Indexer: Matthew Gale
Cover design: Alex Wright
Cover image: shutterstock/Mykola Mazuryk
Typeset by Lapiz Digital Services, Chennai, India

CONTENTS

FIGURES AND TABLES

AUTHORS

Alison Holt is an internationally acclaimed expert in the governance of data and information technology, and sustainability. Alison brings over 30 years of experience of working in the IT industry in the USA, Europe, Australia, New Zealand and, most recently, Papua New Guinea. Delivering excellence across the private and public sector, she specialises in organisational governance, procurement, strategic planning and expediting organisational change programmes through the use of business realisation technologies. Alison is a fellow of both BCS The Chartered Institute for IT and the Institute of IT Professionals, New Zealand, and she was one of the first certified IT professionals in New Zealand. She holds a number of professional memberships, including the NZ Institute of Directors. Alison's first book for the British Computer Society, *Governance of IT* was published in 2013.

Benoit Aubert is a professor at HEC Montréal (Canada) and a fellow of the CIRANO (Center for Interuniversity Research and Analysis on Organizations). His research focuses primarily on governance of information technology (IT), risk management, outsourcing and innovation. He has published extensively on these topics and worked closely with industry to ensure research and practice informed each other. Benoit Aubert's past roles include: director of the Rowe School of Business at Dalhousie University (Canada); head of the School of Information Management and professor at Victoria University of Wellington (New Zealand), where he was the chair of the Spearheading Digital Futures strategic initiative for the university; president and chief executive officer of the CIRANO; and director of research at HEC Montréal.

Geoff Clarke is the chair and expert member of several IT and governance standards committees, and is employed by Microsoft. He works with national standards bodies, government departments and industry experts to ensure that Microsoft and its customers can achieve their strategic goals through the innovative and responsible use of IT. Geoff represents Australia on several international standards committees and contributes to standards on topics such as governance, cloud computing, IT security and artificial intelligence (AI). The common thread through these committees is his focus on providing guidance to organisations on developing data and technology strategies within a robust governance framework. Geoff holds a Bachelor of Commerce degree from the University of Queensland and is a graduate of the Australian Institute of Company Directors. He lives on the Sunshine Coast in Queensland.

Frédéric Gelissen was born in 1970 in Liège (Belgium). When he was 12, he bought the famous Commodore 64, with which he took his first steps into software coding and surfing networks that were not called internet yet. Fred started his professional career in 1995 in a pharmaceutical company. In 2001 he took on the responsibilities of quality and security expert and had his first contact with IT service management (ITSM). This was the spark that started the fire of a strong taste for management and governance. In 2007 he joined a French IT consulting company, where he took the lead of the ITSM, Project and Quality Management team. Then, in 2015 he created PROCSIMA, one of the most successful information security service companies in Belgium. Fred has organised several events for the Belgian ITSMF chapter. It was during one of these that he met the surprising lady, Alison Holt.

Abdelaziz Khadraoui is a scientific collaborator at the University of Geneva. Dr Khadraoui's research relates to the engineering of IT-based services with a specific focus on the engineering of egovernment services and information systems. He is a member of several international conference committees. He is also author or co-author of several contributions and publications in the field of egovernment services and institutional information systems engineering.

Rohan Light works in data governance, strategy and risk. His current projects include practical applications of data trusts, digital regulation (self and other) and issues of probabilistic estimation. His recent body of data work includes openness and transparency, responsible information use and re-identification risk. He is currently focused on de-risking the connections between the Deming–agile family of operational methodologies and common data use/decision-making trips and pratfalls. This is to enable better quality data input to an organisation's machine-learning environment. Based in Te Whanganui-a-Tara Wellington in Aotearoa, New Zealand, he is used to working through complex data governance issues and leveraging the benefits of building open data principles deep into data infrastructure.

Nathalie de Marcellis-Warin is a full professor in the Department of Mathematics and Industrial Engineering at Polytechnique Montréal. She is president and chief executive officer of the CIRANO Research Center. She is also a visiting scientist at Harvard T. Chan School of Public Health and a collaborating member of the Interuniversity Research Centre on Enterprise Networks, Logistics and Transportation (CIRRELT). Holder of a PhD in management science (in risks and insurance management) from École Normale Supérieure de Cachan (France), her research interests focus on risk management and decision making in different risks and uncertainty contexts as well as public policies.

Alisdair McKenzie's career as an IT professional spanned some 50 years in the public and private sectors. He began as an analyst/programmer (COBOL) in 1970 at the NZ Defence EDP Centre and continued on to system requirements development and specification. When he retired from the RNZAF after 20 years as a logistics officer he was engaged as an IT project leader at a motor vehicle assembler. In 1989 he segued into IT auditing, first as a contractor on a major banking system pre-implementation review and then in salaried IT audit roles in public and private enterprises, where he often introduced computer assisted audit techniques. Since the millennium he has practised as an independent consultant on audit and assurance roles, and most recently focused on information security risk management and enterprise cybersecurity governance and management. He is put on guard by the advice of another pale stale male: 'οὐδὲν ἕρπει θνατῶν βιότῳ πάμπολύ γ' ἐκτὸς ἄτας' (Nothing vast enters life without a curse) (Sophocles, *Antigone*, 613–614).

Li Ming was one of the project editors of the second part of the international data governance standard ISO/IEC TR 38505-2:2018 Information technology – Governance of IT – Governance of data – Part 2: Implications of ISO/IEC 38505-1 for data management. His experience from the China Electronic Standardisation Institute and his perspective of technology solutions beyond the world of data management was invaluable as the standard was developed. He currently holds the prestigious role of chair of the IEEE Computer Society Blockchain and Distributed Ledger Standards Committee, the IEEE P2418.2 Standard Data Format for Blockchain Systems and of the IEEE SA P2841 Framework and Process for Deep Learning Evaluation Group. He is also a member of the IEEE Standards Association Review committee, the IEEE SA Asia-Pac Regional Advisory Group and a number of organisations including DAMA and ISACA.

Rose (Rong) Pan, BSI APAC is a chief data governance expert, and member of DAMA, IAPP and BCI. She graduated from Tsinghua University, majoring in computer science, and she continued studying for enterprise strategy and digital transformation at the University of Hong Kong. She is a professional in information security and data governance and co-editor of the ISO 38505 series standard development. In early 2015 she published the book *Big Data Governance and Service*, which first defined a framework of Big Data governance in China. Thus she became a thought leader of data governance. She now leads the team to help Chinese companies attain international privacy compliance to support overseas business, and she also advises the Chinese government on open data, data classification and data sharing.

Beenish Saeed was awarded a Bachelors of Law with Honours from the University of Sussex in 2015 where she was a Chancellor's International Scholar and concentrated on intellectual property, business and Internet laws and regulations. Her passion for Information Technology (IT) literacy stems from the day she received a personal computer at the age of five – her most special present to date. She possesses international legal experience in intellectual property, telecommunications and payment systems. As a Tax and Legal Consultant at Deloitte, Beenish headed up the Pakistani and English student delegations to Harvard University and was awarded for outstanding diplomacy on international development issues in the USA, UK and Belgium. Apart from IT and policy work, Beenish has served in the Royal Navy as an honorary officer cadet. Queen's University awarded a Master of Management, Innovation and Entrepreneurship to Beenish in 2017.

David Sutton's career spans more than 50 years and includes radio transmission, international telephone switching, computing, voice and data networking, information security and critical information infrastructure protection. At Telefónica UK, he was responsible for ensuring the continuity and restoration of the core cellular networks, and represented the company in the electronic communications industry's national resilience forum. In December 2005 he gave evidence to the Greater London Authority enquiry into the mobile telecoms impact of the London bombings. Since retiring from Telefónica UK, he has undertaken a number of critical information infrastructure projects for the European Network and Information Security Agency (ENISA). David has been a member of the BCS Professional Certification Information Security Panel since 2005, and is a co-author of *Information Security Management Principles*, author of *Information Risk Management: A Practitioner's Guide*; and author of *Cyber Security: A Practitioner's Guide*, all published by BCS, The Chartered Institute for IT.

ABBREVIATIONS

AIoT	AI applied to the Internet of Things
BCP	business continuity plan
BI	business intelligence
BPMN	Business Process Model and Notation
CDO	chief data officer
CEO	chief executive officer
CFO	chief financial officer
CIO	chief information officer
DPIA	Data Protection Impact Assessment
DRP	disaster recovery plan
EDM	evaluate, direct, monitor (model)
GDPR	General Data Protection Regulation
HR	human resources
ICT	information and communication technology
IoT	Internet of Things
IT	information technology
ITIL	IT Infrastructure Library®
itSMF	IT Service Management Forum
KPI	key performance indicator
OBASHI®	Ownership, Business Process, Application, System, Hardware, Infrastructure
PDCA	plan, do, check, act
PDF	portable document format
PIA	privacy impact assessment
PII	personally identifiable information
SLA	service level agreement
TOGAF	The Open Group Architecture Framework
UML	Unified Modeling Language

ORGANISATIONAL ABBREVIATIONS

Auto-ISAC   Automotive Information Sharing and Analysis Center
BCI   Business Continuity Institute
BSI   British Standards Institution
DCMS   Department for Digital, Culture, Media & Sport (UK)
ETSI   European Telecommunications Standards Institute
FDA   Food and Drug Administration (US)
FTC   Federal Trade Commission (US)
ISO   International Organization for Standardization
NIST   National Institute of Standards and Technology (US)
OWASP   Open Web Application Security Project
StatsNZ   Statistics New Zealand

PREFACE

Alison Holt

At the time of publication of this book, the world is battling through a global pandemic that has caused havoc and devastation for individuals, families and businesses, and seen entire nations struggle to keep their economies afloat and their health services functioning.

The effects of COVID-19 are raw and painful, and it is too soon to run a 'lessons learnt' exercise to see who made the best use of their data during the pandemic, or to analyse whether any nation's test and trace application performed reliably well, in a way that provided better health outcomes for their population.

What can be said is this: whatever your personal, family, business or national situation, there will always be a 'something' that disturbs your plans – whether that 'something' is a pandemic, an earthquake, a tsunami, a fire, a flood, a gas leak, an extended power outage, a sudden change of government – the list is endless. This book will assist you and your organisation with tools and ideas that will make you more resilient to sudden change. Data is the fuel that powers your business, and if you can harness that power through good governance, you are free to pivot and move quickly and painlessly when your next 'something' event hits.

The aim of this book is to help you on your journey of digital awareness or digital transformation, from wherever your journey starts and whether or not you know your final destination. The book is based around the ISO 38505 series of governance of data standards that have been written for organisations who are contemplating the development and implementation of a data strategy with the aim of delivering new services or products for their customers. Data strategy and digital strategy are becoming increasingly intertwined. Successful delivery of a new data-fuelled app, for example, will require consideration to the hosting infrastructure and organisation's digital strategy. The data strategy should answer the questions: *Where* are we going? *What* are we trying to achieve? *How* does this data strategy fit with the vision, mission and strategy of the organisation? The digital strategy should answer the overarching question: *How* are we are planning to achieve this?

Whether you are just curious at what all the fuss is about data-driven services, or you are wondering how bothered you should be about pairing your intelligent bed or your car to your phone using Bluetooth, through to discovering that you have been given the task of planning and executing a data strategy for your organisation, there is something here for you.

INTRODUCING THE TERMINOLOGY USED IN THIS BOOK

There are multiple definitions available for the following highlighted terms, but for the purposes of this book, terms will be used as explained in the following paragraphs.

Data governance or the **governance of data** are terms that we'll use in the book for the governance activities carried out by a board of directors or trustees, a cabinet committee, or any other top-level group charged with setting policy rules for how their organisations use data for decision making, reference and analysis. We will refer to this group of people as a **governing body**. This governing body is responsible for the development of a **data strategy** to determine how data is used within their organisation to deliver the overarching organisational strategy. Data governance activities can include the actions taken by managers to observe and respect the policy rules set by the governing body, but it should be noted that the data governance duties of the governing body cannot be delegated without a loss of accountability.

Although technically the term **data** refers to the streams of 1s and 0s that, when decoded, convey **information** in the form of words, letters and numbers, we often find ourselves using the term data to refer to the information contained within an electronic filing cabinet, a **database**.

Big Data is a term that has fallen into misuse, with organisations claiming they use Big Data when they often just mean lots of data. If you are dealing with such large volumes of data that you cannot handle them through normal means, then you probably are working with Big Data. That is to say, if you are collecting and storing large and/or expanding volumes of data from one or multiple sources that cannot be processed using your existing traditional data processing application software, then you are using Big Data.

While we are dealing with the more confusing of the terms, we will introduce **digital**. In common use, the terms 'data' and 'digital' are muddled, but we will try to stick to **data systems** for a content-related context and **digital systems** for a hardware or infrastructure-related context. Data sits on digital systems, which follow the design principles laid out in a **digital strategy**. **Data products** and **data services** are easier to define, with a data service being the intangible version of a data product.

Managing data falls in the realm of the **data manager**, although overall responsibility for all things data may lie with a **chief data officer** (CDO). The data manager has a close relationship with the data he or she manages, and a responsibility to make sure that the **data quality** and other characteristics of the data are fit for purpose with the organisational use of data. **Data management** tasks include putting in place the tools, frameworks, storage facilities, policies, practices, systems and so on to ensure that data is accessible and available in line with organisational requirements, as defined and stipulated by the **data owners**. **Data stewards** sound as though they might also be data managers, but their role is more focused on championing the correct use of data and protecting against unauthorised use. Ironically, the data stewards in an organisation generally spend more of their time with the people (data users) than the data itself.

INTRODUCING THE AUTHORS

As the editor of this book, it has been my great pleasure to invite my international colleagues, who are governance of data subject matter experts, to each write a guest chapter. Most of the authors have had direct experience of developing national and international standards, and they have all had exciting careers. Some of these careers are shorter than others – the youngest author is in her 30s and the oldest is in his 70s.

The book contains contributions from colleagues based in Australia, Belgium, Canada, China, New Zealand, Papua New Guinea and the United Kingdom. The resulting book provides a richness of experience from different areas of the world and different generational perspectives.

As a group of authors, we have decided collectively to donate all royalties from this book to charity.

INTRODUCING THE STANDARDS REFERRED TO IN THIS BOOK

Most of the authors associated with this book have been involved in some capacity in the development of International Organization for Standardization (ISO) standards, so it shouldn't come as any surprise that the theory behind the book sits across the following prominent standards:

- ISO/DIS 37000: Guidance for the Governance of Organisations (in development at the time of writing)
- ISO/IEC 38500:2015 Information technology – Governance of IT for the organisation
- ISO/IEC 38505-1:2017 Information technology – Governance of IT – Governance of data – Part 1: Application of ISO/IEC 38500 to the governance of data
- ISO/IEC TR 38505-2:2018 Information technology – Governance of IT – Governance of data – Part 2: Implications of ISO/IEC 38505-1 for data management.

The titles of international standards can be a bit overwhelming, so we will generally refer to them by their numbers.

37000

The scope of the developing 37000 standard is the governance of organisations, and the current draft (at time of publication) provides 11 principles of good governance for setting up a comprehensive governance framework in line with external legislative and regulatory requirements. The aim of 37000 is to assist with the development of a governance framework that will enable an organisation to reflect its purpose and mission to external stakeholders and society in general, and to drive organisational accountability and effectiveness.

38500

The governance of IT standard 38500 pre-dates the governance of organisations standards, and it includes a list of six governance principles and guidance for the development of a governance framework for IT.

38505 – Parts 1 and 2

These governance of data standards sit within the IT governance framework described in 38500. They form the basis of this book and will be described in greater detail in Chapter 3.

NAVIGATING THE BOOK

Acknowledging the wide diversity of audience for the book and the very different styles of our guest authors, we have developed a 'tube map' representation of chapters with suggested pathways for different readers. Feel free to hop in and out of the book as best suits your needs.

Key chapters for key roles

Although most people reading this book will find most chapters relevant, we thought it would be helpful to know which chapters would be particularly useful for a specific role. Table 0.1 is a quick look-up table for busy people reading this book between meetings.

Table 0.1 Key chapters

Key chapters	Route A Data curious	Route B Policy writers	Route C Managers	Route D CDO	Route E Governing body
1	■			■	■
2	■			■	■
3		■		■	■
4	■	■		■	■
5			■	■	■
6			■	■	■
7	■		■	■	■
8			■	■	■
9			■	■	
10			■	■	
11			■	■	
12			■	■	
Appendix A		■		■	

Figure 0.1 The tube map for this book

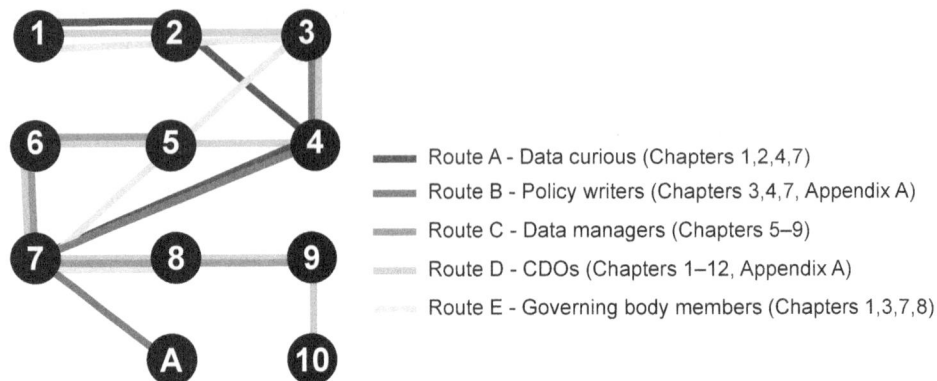

Route A - Data curious (Chapters 1,2,4,7)
Route B - Policy writers (Chapters 3,4,7, Appendix A)
Route C - Data managers (Chapters 5–9)
Route D - CDOs (Chapters 1–12, Appendix A)
Route E - Governing body members (Chapters 1,3,7,8)

PLANNING YOUR JOURNEY

Though most of the book will be practical to all, the 'tube map' in Figure 0.1 provides a route through chapters of particular interest for the following roles.

Route A for the data curious

Typically, you don't consider yourself really interested in technology or IT systems, but you are aware that things are changing around you. You are enjoying the convenience of some data-enabled services – such as being able to book and track a taxi or a pizza from your phone or being able to rent out your spare bedroom on an ad hoc basis. Maybe, though, you have heard some horror stories of telephone companies inadvertently releasing bank details and you are wondering who you should be sharing your information with? Or perhaps you are having to give the same information again and again to different parts of the same organisation, and you're wondering why?

This book will raise some questions to ask of data service providers, and some things to look for in a trusted service.

Route B for the policy writers

As a policy writer you have been tasked with writing policy around data, maybe specifically addressing privacy legislation such as the General Data Protection Regulation (GDPR). (The implementation of the GDPR in 2016 raised awareness for organisations across the world to develop data policy that would determine how they would handle personal data. Although the GDPR is part of European Union law, it has had global influence in the development of national data protection and privacy law.)

This book will provide support in writing data policy that addresses the compliance needs of your organisation.

Route C for the managers

Managers have a vital role in the area of the governance of data, to advise and support a board that is planning digital transformation, in understanding what is possible immediately and also what could be possible in the future.

This book will provide support in implementing a data strategy.

Route D for the CDO

As CDO, you have responsibility for all things data at a senior executive level. It is likely that you came up through a data/technology career path, but it is unlikely that you still have direct hands-on access to data in your CDO role.

This book will assist with setting practice direction.

Route E for governing body members (directors, etc.)

Members of a governing body have the role of setting digital strategy and also responsibility for the use of data throughout their organisation.

This book will assist with developing a digital strategy and guidance for setting appropriate policy to ensure that the strategy is carried out.

And now, with all the introductions out of the way, let's get on with the book.

PART 1
THE REQUIREMENT TO GOVERN DATA

I asked Siri™ 'What is data?' and Siri's response was, 'Interesting question.' Yes, Siri, it is an interesting question.

This first part of the book will provide some background into data and why it holds such an important role in our lives. We'll look at the benefits of collecting and sharing data and why governing data is an essential task for all organisations.

WHAT IS DATA?

We tend to think of data in electronic form, but humans were collecting data thousands of years before computers. Although this book will focus on the governance of data in electronic form, we will start off by looking at the history of the collection of data. The governance practices applied to the collection of data in physical form (from clay tiles through knotted ropes to paper) will shed light on our approach to the governance of data held in electronic form. Although our media for storage has changed, the issues faced by our forebears will be very familiar.

History also reveals the significant advantage that can be gained from holding the right data of the right quality at the right time, where 'right' is a statement of fit for purpose. Whether you are looking for an advantage over your competitors, or finding a cure for a disease or looking to find patterns in physical phenomena or events, then the 'right' data is your friend. Putting in place a governance framework will ensure that this 'right' data is in the right place at the right time.

DATA GOVERNANCE OR DATA MANAGEMENT?

We often confuse the terms data governance and data management. This isn't surprising, given that some major countries in the world do not have a term for data governance and it sort of 'translates' as data management. The governance of data, or data governance, covers the evaluation of what needs to be done, providing direction to make it happen and monitoring to check that the desired outcomes have been delivered. Data governance can be extended to include: the application and operationalisation of the governance of data; and the setting of policy to ensure that the desired outcomes will be met through management outputs, the establishment of controls, and controlling mechanisms to ensure that the governance requirements are met.

Data management is the administration of data and includes, among other activities, the setting up of databases, the transfer of data and the archiving of data.

1

1   DATA COLLECTION THROUGH THE AGES

Alison Holt

For thousands of years humans have collected, stored, reported on, made decisions with, distributed and disposed of data. Amazingly, some of these data sets are still accessible today. They reveal information about ancient civilisations that would otherwise remain a mystery. Their original purpose, however, was not to provide a journal entry or historical record, but to inform the decision makers of the day.

CENSUS DATA

The Babylonians were collecting census data over 4000 years ago to work out how much food was needed to feed the population. Their census records took the form of clay tiles, and several of these tiles are held in the British Museum. Around 1500 years later, the Egyptians and the Chinese started to collect census data. The Egyptians used their data to plan the workforce needed for the building of pyramids and for the assignment of land after the annual flooding of the Nile. The Chinese census of 2 AD collected data from a staggering 57.67 million people from 12.36 million households. Meanwhile, over in Europe, the Romans were collecting census data every five years to estimate taxes due, through a sort of early rating system. The Roman method of census collection was unusually disruptive, especially for heavily pregnant mothers married to out-of-towners. It involved every man and his family returning to his place of birth to be counted.

Skipping another thousand years, we come to the production of the Domesday Book in England, a detailed survey of land holding, wealth and population across the country to enable determination of tax, rents and military service obligations of the populace, from the lowly peasants through to the barons. Five hundred years later, we find the Incas collecting census data by knotting ropes made from alpaca or llama hair.

Finally, from the 1800s we have a number of countries around the world collecting census data on a regular basis to inform not just the taxable liability of their citizens, but to assist with the building of houses, schools and hospitals, and eventually to inform programmes for the eradication of disease.

Governance lessons from census data

Census data is generally well governed and provides some interesting insights into the successful governance of data, and the need for influential and determined data custodians. UK census data cannot be released for 100 years, and the Census Registrars General through the ages have had to fight off requests for access. In the early 1900s, a request from the sanitation authorities for access to personal information in the 1891 census was denied, citing personally identifiable information (PII) reasons and the undertaking of confidentiality at the point of data collection. I suspect the requesters would have argued that many lives could have been saved, or at least improved, through the release of the data. More recently, there were online petitions in the UK for the release of the 1921 census data to assist family historians trace their ancestors. The Census Act of 1920 made the release of this information before 2021 not just ill-advised, but illegal.

Retention of data has been a trying subject for the Census Registrars General, who have several times struggled for the preservation of records, and for adequate fire-proof and water-proof storage facilities. There have also been arguments over the appropriateness of some of the data collected, and issues with the time taken to process and analyse census data. The 1911 Census of England and Wales collected information on the fertility of women in marriage, to help understand issues with the falling birth rate amidst the need for a growing workforce to support industrial expansion, but it was 1923 before a final report could be published on the data. The time delay in receiving this information must have been a great source of frustration for the initiator of the report. Timeliness is an important factor that needs to be taken into account when considering data quality.

The automation of processing and collection of census data has been a slow process, starting with the use of punched cards in the US 1890 Census to speed up the analysis of census responses. Back in 1890, processing using punched cards was calculated to be 10 times faster than the previous manual process. Since then, electronic analysis of census data has blossomed, but putting confidence in the electronic collection of census data has been a matter of debate for many years. In preparation for the 2018 New Zealand Census of Population and Dwellings, Statistics New Zealand (StatsNZ) modernised the process for data collection; according to their website:

> We designed the 2018 Census forms primarily for online completion. Our aim was for 70 percent of respondents to complete their census online. The online forms were designed to work on a range of devices, from personal computers to smartphones, and were easier to complete. The version for smartphones was a first for the census, intended to encourage young people (aged 15–24 years) to take part. The 2018 Census forms were available online and in paper, in English and te reo Māori.
>
> (Stats.govt.nz 2019)

Of course, collecting data electronically brings a completely new set of requirements for a data governance framework for the census. These types of framework will be the focus of this book.

Census data has always been collected by people who care passionately about data and understand the importance of collecting data in a consistent way. My StatsNZ friends and colleagues involved in the census in New Zealand have taken on the role of guardians protecting a precious asset – and rightly so. Census development and data collection is the gold standard among population surveys. Being supported by legislation helps to focus the respondents on completing the questions, and picking one night in every three or five years to hold the census gives the survey a sense of awe and mystery, akin with election night and Christmas Eve. There are few other sectors and areas where the importance of collecting consistent, quality data and the value of that data is understood so well, but health is one of these.

HEALTH DATA

Without data, how can we determine the difference between an isolated incident and an epidemic? How do we know how effective vaccination, chemotherapy, specific surgical procedures and so on are unless we measure outcomes accurately across a statistically significant sample of the population? If we can't determine what causes the spread of infection, how can we fight an epidemic? And, once we've worked out how infection is spread, how do we contact the people who we think could be vulnerable?

There have been a number of examples in the last few years where data scientists have worked alongside health professionals to protect populations. COVID-19 aside, the Ebola outbreak in 2014 is an example of this – a disease that initially had no antidote, no vaccination to provide protection. It was essential to quickly understand how the disease was spread, and to identify potential carriers and who they had been in contact with. Data was the key in unlocking the facts that would give health professionals and government officials an understanding of how the outbreak could be stemmed. One of the Ebola stories that stuck in my mind was the health care worker who had been caring for an infected patient and who then took a commercial flight across the US. The following day she developed a fever that resulted in her being moved into isolation, tested for and then treated for Ebola. Working out who was on the plane with her, and therefore potentially at risk, was straightforward. Working out how she got infected, and who else she had been in contact with along the way, was trickier. The incident resulted in a need to rethink the governance of data relating to disease.

Let's look at vaccination data: the Gates Foundation has done the most amazing job of vaccinating against polio, with the aim of eradicating the disease. They work by collecting data and carrying out analysis. How can we know what is really killing children in the poorest areas of the world unless we can collect, analyse and interpret data? In New Zealand we are seeing the re-emergence of diseases that had been 'eradicated'. How can we address the root cause of this issue without reliable data to inform us?

Data 'demonstrating' a link between autism and vaccination has put mothers off having their babies vaccinated. We've had recent measles and whooping cough epidemics. How ironic that babies should be suffering in first world countries, having been withdrawn from vaccination programmes, while third world babies are happily surviving through recently established vaccination programmes.

Similarly, data 'demonstrating' that a tsunami defence system would protect a length of the Japanese coastline led to deaths in the major earthquake of March 2011. People in the affluent areas, who thought they were fully protected by the tsunami defence system, had insufficient time to run for safety when the defence system was overwhelmed. The people of the poorer coastal towns that didn't have a defence system in place ran for the hills as soon as they knew that the tsunami was coming, and survived.

Governance lessons from health data

Health data has traditionally been well governed, in the sense that, since health records were first collected, all stakeholders have understood the value of having data made accessible to them, the privacy risk of sharing data and the constraints set by legislation, local health boards and policy.

TRADITIONAL DATA-HEAVY INDUSTRIES

Certain industries are (and always have been) heavily dependent on data, and the survival of individual companies and the reputation of individual government agencies within those industries have fully depended on their ability to safely collect and store data. Examples are police forces, airlines, schools, warehouses, prisons, supermarkets and companies and government agencies involved in defence and military applications. These organisations traditionally collected information on paper and spreadsheets, but now I can check into a flight online and order my weekly supermarket shop without leaving the house; and the New Zealand police force, for example, carry iPads and iPhones on the street and work with real time information.

Back in the 1990s I ran a project with a private school in the UK to demonstrate the use of databases to Year 5 and Year 6 (10- and 11-year-old) students. As part of the project we visited a supermarket and looked at the bar codes, stock control and logistics. The supermarket data was highly accurate, and the shop knew how many items had been sold that week and what needed to be restocked. Both overstocking and understocking caused issues. The system controlling the stock was reasonably straightforward and was most likely hosted in the supermarket chain's IT centre, for internal staff access only. It didn't take into account the multiple channels of data that would be combined to predict demand today, and it wouldn't have been able to support services such as online shopping or specials based on loyalty card usage.

In May 2016 a group of us presented at an international governance of data conference in Suzhou, China. We spoke to a member of the Chinese Securities Regulatory Commission afterwards and learnt of the huge volumes (measured in petabytes) of transactional data that he dealt with on a daily basis, and we began to understand his requirement for a governance framework that would protect his high-speed and high-accuracy data transfers.

Many traditional industries, such as food stores and financial markets, started off with paper and pens and verbal or written governance processes for what could be transferred where and when. These industries now trade almost entirely electronically, collecting large volumes of data from and sharing large volumes of data with multiple sources. There is a need for governance frameworks to ensure that the same level of rigour that was associated with traditional business methods is now applied to maximise the value and protect the data at the heart of each modern business.

Governance lessons from traditional data-heavy industries

Some of our data-heavy industries have been the slowest to take the opportunity of driving new value from their data through Big Data techniques. We cannot assume that because our organisation handles large volumes of data that it has embraced the benefits of new technology, cheaper processing and storage. Collecting and processing large volumes of data without the application of governance principles can open up risks, including an exposure to non-compliance to legislation. The concept of Big Data demonstrates the potential for providing access to petabytes of data to search for patterns or solutions. For medical researchers looking for the cause of an infrequent medical occurrence, or financial analysts looking for global spending trends, the access to Big Data is often a key to solving problems that have been outstanding for decades. Making assumptions from poor-quality data (where quality is measured as a requirement to provide reliable results) would lead to disastrous consequences. Successful Big Data users have put in place the necessary governance measures to ensure that they are working from data that is fit for purpose, and not unnecessarily collecting data that is not relevant.

When data storage dropped significantly in price, it was common for organisations, spurred on by the concept of Big Data, to collect all the data they could because they could. There was little thought to the consequences of collecting data of mixed quality to inform decision making or the consequence of unnecessarily collecting PII. As the area of Big Data has matured and found its niche market, most organisations have settled into collecting the data they need – and only the data they need.

MODERN DAY DATA-ENABLED BUSINESSES

The modern day data-enabled business has an even greater need for a clear governance framework. Many business start-ups are treading new ground and do not have the benefit of the traditional practices for governance.

Let's suppose that I am starting up a business that prints three dimensional (3D) widgets and delivers them by drone, or I am launching a fleet of driverless taxis. Where do I start to put in place a governance of data framework that will enhance the value of my business while reducing the risks for all the stakeholders involved and ensuring that the business is run within legislative constraints?

At the time of going to press, Netflix is testing measures to prevent account holders sharing their account password beyond physical household members.[1] Good data governance can protect the revenue from data services and products.

Governance lessons from modern day data-enabled businesses

We have seen a number of start-up data-empowered businesses get up and running very quickly, delivering value to their users and customers in innovative ways, but in some cases these businesses have not considered the risk and constraints associated with the delivery of their new service or product. For example, a common mistake is to inadvertently provide a data set that, when combined with a second easily available data set, can reveal information that disadvantages the target users and customers. An example of this was a property data application that provided useful land information on houses for sale, and value to estate agents, house sellers and house purchasers. However, a second organisation combined the property data with freely available police data, and was able to show the crime levels at each address.

---

1   https://www.wired.com/story/netflix-password-sharing-crackdown/

SUMMARY

While the technology sector leaps from one buzzword to another, presenting the latest emerging trend, it is easy to forget that humans have been collecting information and processing data since the beginning of time. Our foundation for data governance is shaped by the civilisations that have come before us. There are valuable lessons to learn by reflecting on previous uses of data through the ages, and by looking at the varying approaches to data collection from different sectors. Specifically, the leaders of the most successful civilisations were quick to work out what data to collect and how that data could be shared by working through the incentives and disincentives of collecting and sharing the data available to them.

2 INCENTIVES AND DISINCENTIVES FOR COLLECTING AND SHARING DATA

Alison Holt

There have always been incentives for collecting and sharing data, but only recently has it been easy to move data around and analyse the results. The benefits from sharing data are enormous and can inform a healthier, safer world: by quickly processing accident data, we can help to prevent the accident recurring; by sharing information on the treatment of Ebola or COVID-19 patients, we can assist drug companies with building a vaccine or a drug to treat the disease, and we can help to develop processes to prevent the spread of the disease.

On the other hand, there can be negative consequences of collecting and sharing data. As data storage has become cheaper and processing power has increased over the last 10 years, we have seen organisations collecting data sets from multiple sources and making decisions based on this data without considering that the data sets might not be of equal value or quality or accuracy. We have also seen data sharing that has ended up with negative consequences, typically where an organisation has made information publicly available in a safe way without realising that combining their information with another publicly available data source inadvertently reveals confidential or secure information. A good data governance framework will assist our organisation in collecting and sharing data to drive value without breaking privacy or delivering any other unintended consequences.

A MATTER OF TRUST

We have always shared data with those we trust: the family doctor, our solicitor, our bank, our children's schools and so on. Now we are sharing data with those who will not provide a service or a product unless we share our information. There are invisible electronic barriers that we need to cross: we need to be above a certain age to purchase alcohol and under a certain age to get insurance. We are asked to divulge common identifiers such as our address, our date of birth, our bank numbers, and we are asked to provide answers to secret questions that only we should know the answer to. Some of my more security conscious friends and colleagues have invented names and birthdays, and partner names. That in itself carries the risk of being found out by the wife/husband as you are typing in the name of your pretend partner, or just simply forgetting your fictional birth date.

A couple of years ago I was interviewing applicants with a colleague and we found the perfect candidate for the job. She was well presented, erudite, personable and full of energy. Our human resources (HR) manager ran some checks and discovered that our perfect candidate was operating under three identities.

I know of two other Alison Holts with email accounts from the same provider, and I occasionally get their email. One is a soccer mom and the other is an embroiderer, so it is generally pretty obvious that I'm not the intended recipient. My preferred rental car company invoiced me for a car hired by an Australian in the US, who happened to use my company code instead of his own. The Australian paid for the car with his own credit card, and as far as the hire car company were concerned 'nothing happened'. However, I have his full name and address details (from my invoice) and I suspect that he has my details (from his invoice).

The stakes for sharing data are getting higher, and yet in many places we see that individuals and companies are operating under outdated governance principles with outdated processes for data handling. There is a 'we'll be fine' mindset to security that is troubling. In a rush to download the latest application we hastily say yes to terms and conditions whose consequences we do not take time to understand. In a rush to get a product to market, we overlook the line in the hosting contract that defines the ownership and access to our data. We assume that we will always have access to our data. We often don't stop to consider that our freely downloaded application could be selling our data to third parties.

Our customers select passwords that are easy to guess and when we enforce strong passwords, then, inevitably, our customers write them down. We cannot change the way we do business without changing the governance structure that controls our business and without considering the consequences of our changes. My father was convinced that, when engineers started to rely on computers for calculating the stresses and strains on structures such as bridges, they lost the sense of order of magnitude that they once needed when they used slide rules. We are changing the way that data flows in and out of an organisation and how it is used to drive or support new services and products, and we need to keep an eye on the consequences of these changes and develop a governance framework that will support the new ways of working and business delivery.

IMPACT FOR DIRECTORS

If you are a member of a board reading this book, you might be asking yourself at this juncture: 'Why do directors need to care about data? Surely data is the responsibility of the management team?' Well, let's explore this.

It could be fatal for your business if you totally ignored the 'data boom' while your competitors took full advantage of it. At best, you would miss out on the ability to reduce costs through offering smarter services. You might end up purchasing data-driven services and products from your competitors to support your business and, at worst, you could lose your reputation and entire customer base to your competitors. Businesses ignoring the potential for data-led insights could suffer revenue loss and unnecessary exposure to risk.

Customers are as interested in the means of delivering the service or product as they are in the actual service or product. Drone delivery might be a passing gimmick, but recognising and remembering your customers' preferences drives loyalty and returning customers. The ability to track my product as it is being delivered is very attractive and it reduces the number of phone calls I will make to the organisation providing the product. If I do need to call my service or product provider, I'm going to appreciate the organisation that has put effort into understanding calling patterns and external factors that affect call volumes and has staff available as required to meet predicted load. I'm also going to have a preference for the organisation that can handle repair and maintenance efficiently – especially if either myself or the purchased product are sited in a remote location.[*]

As a customer of government services, I am interested in my government agencies sharing data so that I don't have to re-enter pages of information every time I sign up for a new service. At the same time, I am very keen that my personal data isn't hacked into or stolen, left on a CD on a train, or erroneously distributed by email.

OPPORTUNITIES FOR THE DATA-DRIVEN BUSINESS

There are many examples of traditional businesses benefitting from the data boom and the new data devices and technology options available. Think Internet of Things (IoT) technologies, smart city projects, smart meters for electricity, driverless cars, drones and companies such as Uber, Airbnb and so on. It could be daunting for the traditional business wondering how to get started, but it's more straightforward than it looks. There are some great case studies of traditional businesses that have taken on a new data service (such as restaurants that added the ability to track food delivery) or a new data product (such as marine companies introducing automated monitoring for maintenance planning of remote devices). For some of these traditional companies dabbling in data-driven innovation, they have been rewarded with not just benefits for their businesses but also the opportunity to deliver their new services to their competitors.

There is also the opportunity to address long-standing problems and issues that have stumped scientists and researchers in the past. If you are a research company, then it is worth revisiting the value you can extract from your data using the latest extraction and data integration techniques. In 2013, neonatal babies were dying from simple infections with no obvious pattern that would alert individual hospitals to what was going on. A Big Data study that collected hospital monitoring records showed that the babies who died had a raised temperature one day that dropped back to normal the next day, but then the following day the temperature would spike and by then it was too late to treat the baby. This study prompted hospitals to start giving antibiotics to neonatal babies at the first sign of a raised temperature, and the death rate dropped dramatically.

RISK

New data services and data products are designed to deliver specified outcomes, but will also often deliver unintended outcomes.

Some of these unintended outcomes will be favourable and add to the value of the new service or product, for example a data service that was originally intended for operating electronic bail and enabling home detention of minor offenders was repurposed at the start of the COVID-19 pandemic as a quarantine compliance application.

Some will result in negative consequences that need to be addressed through the organisational risk programme, for example social media applications have enabled us to reconnect with long lost school and college friends and to stay connected with family and friends travelling or living overseas, yet the unintended negative consequences are significant. An article by Mayo Clinic Staff from December 2019 describes the positive and negative affect of social media use on teenagers. The article describes the harmful effects as

> distracting them, disrupting their sleep, and exposing them to bullying, rumour spreading, unrealistic views of other people's lives and peer pressure.
> (Mayo Clinic Staff 2019)

An extreme example of social media used with negative consequences was reported in March 2019, when the city of Christchurch, New Zealand, was terrorised by a gunman and footage of the killings was circulating rapidly through social media. The ABC news site reported that

> New Zealand Prime Minister Jacinda Ardern has taken Facebook to task for failing to remove graphic vision of the Christchurch shootings from its platforms, while vowing to "give the gunman nothing, not even his name."
> (ABC.net.au 2019)

Before you adopt or release any new data service or product, consider the potential negative uses or outcomes, and raise these with the organisational risk manager.

REGULATION

To date, many governments and regulators have been slow in providing guidance and regulation to support management boards of enterprises in discharging their duties in respect of governance of data – although the GDPR implemented in 2018, with its global reach, provides incentives for boards to understand their accountability to their customers and users. In particular, the GDPR has helped to raise awareness in boards for their responsibility should their organisation experience a significant breach of data security/privacy. Over the last few years, many devices and applications have been developed with serious security shortcomings, but consequences for non-compliance with regulation should encourage boards to take a more active role in the governance of data.

On a more positive note, recent developments show some useful guidance now being issued by governments, industry vertical groupings and IT professional groups. For example, the website of the Office of the Privacy Commissioner of New Zealand provides guidance and links to many useful resources (https://www.privacy.org.nz/).

SUMMARY

With regulation such as the GDPR (or national equivalent privacy legislation) becoming more widely adopted, and countries around the world updating privacy and data protection legislation to address emerging threats, directors need to know that they have sound data governance in place that can meet requirements for compliance. Good governance isn't just about meeting compliance needs, though; it is about creating the environment for a business to thrive and grow. Good governance of data enables directors to provide the environment to support data innovation. The next chapter describes a set of documents providing internationally endorsed guidance to assist directors in putting in place good governance of data for their organisations.

3   THE THEORY BEHIND GOVERNING DATA

Alison Holt

Back in 2015 I was part of a group of international subject matter experts working on governance standards. Together we recognised a need for international guidelines to assist organisations in assessing the value and risk of data use, and in developing and implementing a data strategy. As a group we saw huge benefits to organisations embracing the data boom.

We had just begun to see several innovative companies developing new data-enabled products and services to enhance the experiences of their customers, and new format companies (such as Uber and Airbnb) developing traditional infrastructure services with no traditional infrastructure. Instead, they built international services based on data collection and matching customer needs to available providers.

However, we also observed that the newspapers were full of stories where lack of governance led to costly exposures. There were examples of telecommunications chief executive officers (CEOs) who didn't know whether their stolen customer data had been encrypted, toy manufacturers who were storing personal conversations with young children, companies on-selling user data without the knowledge of the users and so on.

Data sovereignty was a hot topic, and there was a drive within nations to control data as if it could not pass international borders. Misunderstandings among influential data users led to the building of expensive data centres in-country to house data that was subsequently transferred without any protection around the world. Even highly intelligent individuals were struggling with the concept of data in the cloud, and considered a 'cloud service provider' as something relating to the weather.

We had witnessed this rigid national border thinking before, when we were developing an international standard for the governance of digital forensics. Information relating to a crime could cross international borders and move between two jurisdictions where the handling of information relating to a crime could be very different. We noticed a huge difference in the handling of information in nations that had recent experience in terrorism. The aim of the digital forensics governance standard was to establish an international framework that could be followed in all jurisdictions and support a uniform, forensic investigation behind an international crime.

Similarly, we considered that providing international guidance for the governance of data would enable nations to have confidence in not just storing their data overseas but also in the transfer and processing of that data, wherever that should occur.

However, standards are not always looked on favourably by governing bodies. They can be seen as representing yet another compliance hoop that has to be jumped through. The advantage of following an international standard is that you can encourage your partners and suppliers to adhere to the same guidance. Organisations can have trust and confidence in a hosting service, for example, that can demonstrate compliance to the IT Service Management and IT Security Management standards without the need to send a delegation to visit the centre.

International (ISO) standards are produced by diverse groups, with representatives from different nations (at least five represented in a standards working group and up to 164 nations participating in reviewing) and different organisational types (corporates, government agencies, not-for-profits, charities, independent consultants, universities, etc.). ISO standards go through a staged development process, with formal national ballots at each stage. Although the process can seem tedious to outsiders, there is huge benefit from the international consensus approach in that it generally delivers final standards that can work and have meaning anywhere in the world. The balloting process at each stage ensures quality control over the content in the standard and international appropriateness of the guidance provided.

National standards bodies take the advice of their country subject matter experts and can vote yes or no to a standard moving forward a stage. For the governance of data standards, we had 32 participating (voting) nations and 12 observer nations. If a nation votes yes, they have the option of adding comments as to where the standard could be improved. If they vote no, they must add comments to show where the standard could be improved. Assuming that the developing standard passes a stage ballot (which involves getting sufficient positive votes and fewer than the maximum allowed negative votes), then the standard document goes to a ballot resolution meeting chaired by the project editor. At this meeting, the project editor must address each comment and suggest how the document has been amended to account for it. Alternatively, the editor must give a reason for not accepting the comment. As I recount the process, I can already hear you beginning to yawn, but I want to establish that you can have confidence in using our final published documents.

As a director myself, I was particularly keen that we created a series of standards that were useful and presented in a practical and accessible way. I was also keen that we kicked off with a principle-based standard outlining the theory behind good governance of data, but that we followed this up with a practical implementation guide with case studies to demonstrate how organisations had followed the theory and how they had benefitted from it.

So far we have two parts to the series (available from www.iso.org):

- ISO/IEC 38505-1:2017 Information technology – Governance of IT – Governance of data – Part 1: Application of ISO/IEC 38500 to the governance of data

- ISO/IEC TR 38505-2:2018 Information technology – Governance of IT – Governance of data – Part 2: Implications of ISO/IEC 38505-1 for data management

There are plans in place to add to the series, including a standard on data classification and terminology. This will be particularly helpful in applying definitions to terms that are being used inconsistently – such as 'Big Data'.

38505-1 APPLICATION OF ISO/IEC 38500 TO THE GOVERNANCE OF DATA

ISO/IEC 38505-1:2017 Information technology – Governance of IT – Governance of data – Part 1: Application of ISO/IEC 38500 to the governance of data (available at https://www.iso.org/standard/56639.html), takes the governance of IT theory from ISO/IEC 38500:2015 Information technology – Governance of IT for the organisation and applies the principles and model to data. The ISO Governance of IT standard was first published in 2008 and provides a set of six principles and a model to show how the governing body interacts with the management body. The six governance principles identified in 38500 are as follows:

- responsibility;
- strategy;
- acquisition;
- performance;
- conformance;
- human behaviour.

The overarching ISO Governance of IT standard (38500) presents these principles as essential elements for a governing body to consider when developing a governance framework for IT. Once *responsibility* for IT has been assigned, it is key for an organisation to develop *strategy* that ensures that all IT activities are aligned with the vision and mission of the organisation, and can be re-aligned as an organisation develops and evolves. The principle of *acquisition* ensures that IT procurement aligns with organisational requirements and policy. *Conformance* ensures compliance with legislation, internal policy and any other relevant regulatory or ethical frameworks. *Performance* ensures that IT provision meets the requirements of the organisation, recognising the unnecessary expense of overperformance and the lost hours from underperformance. And, finally, the *human behaviour* principle encourages consideration of all the people involved in the delivery and use of IT systems, whatever their role.

The Governance of IT standard also provides a model that shows the activities of the governing body in determining IT strategy with external input, developing policy and directing activities and monitoring to ensure that the IT function is delivered in a way that supports the vision, goals and culture of the organisation. In the 38500 model, the governing body is shown as evaluating, directing and monitoring activities (the EDM model), and the managers, on the receiving end of this direction, are shown as managing the operational and developmental aspects of IT systems, and reporting back to the governing body. Traditionally, we think of the managers following a plan, do, check, act (PDCA) model, and we can visualise how the two models (EDM and PDCA) intersect, where direction results in plan and do, and check and act feed into monitoring.

Just about everybody in an organisation interacts with IT systems as a tool or as a supporting element to enable them to carry out their role. IT systems need to be available as and when required, and if they underperform or overperform or fail to enable the organisation to meet legislative requirements, then they cause problems. For most of the time, IT systems that are well chosen, maintained and supported are invisible to their users. Data is different. For most staff in an organisation, it is data that informs their role, or data created by them that informs the organisation. Data of too high a quality can be an unnecessary expense, depending on how it is created and maintained, and data of too low a quality can lead to poor decisions. Poor-quality data can also affect revenue, increase costs, increase risk exposure and so on. Poor decision making is just one unwanted consequence of poor-quality data. Data is the fuel for the engine of an organisation and, without it, organisations drift and stall.

Data is not a subset of IT, but an element that needs to be considered in its own right. It needs to be looked at with a different lens from IT. The focus of an IT strategy is generally about planning resources for the next three to five years, with a heavy emphasis on security management and availability. The focus of a data strategy is more likely to be over a shorter time span, as opportunities for data-driven services come and go at a fast rate. The accelerated rate of the development of enabling technology means that data services can be continually enhanced and built upon, as costs to deliver services reduce and as data collections grow and new patterns emerge. It occurred to us as standards editors that we should pinpoint the particular areas where governance was needed, and we developed a data accountability map to show this.

The data accountability map

The data accountability map shows six areas of focus where governance in the form of direction, evaluation and monitoring is required:

- **Collect:** determining the point(s) where data is collected from internal or external sources, from the organisation or from agents acting on behalf of the organisation.
- **Store:** determining whether that should be in-house or external, in-country or overseas for the different data types collected.
- **Report:** understanding how data can be analysed and manipulated to provide accurate reports.
- **Decide:** using data to inform decisions.
- **Distribute:** determining how and when and to whom data should be distributed.
- **Dispose:** determining how and when and where data should be disposed.

We realised that highlighting the areas where data governance should be applied was useful, but there was still a jump required to take these areas and create a meaningful governing body plan or strategy for data. Although governance is not all about creating a strategy, we saw that creating a data strategy would be a vital first step for a governing body to drive a consolidated organisational approach to using data.

We didn't want to make the guidance all about risk and scaremongering, but we also didn't want directors to ignore relevant legislation and their own internal compliance requirements. We wanted the emphasis to be on the value that can be released from putting in place good governance.

The standard provides three considerations to be applied at each point in the data accountability map. The first consideration is **value** – what is the value that can be derived at this particular point? The second is **risk** – what are the risks associated with this activity? And thirdly we invite our governors and directors to consider **constraints** in the form of legislation and internal policy and values that might constrain the use of data. The considerations are presented in a matrix against the six points of the data accountability map with examples of how they can be applied. A governing body can work through the matrix using the example questions and add sector or industry specific questions.

By the time a governing body has worked through Part 1 of the 38505 standard, the directors should have a data strategy in place, and a clear idea of how they can govern the use of data throughout their organisation so as to achieve the organisational vision and mission and follow the overall strategy. They will have assessed how much of a data-driven business they want to be, and they will have identified areas where policy needs to be put in place to meet organisational goals while also protecting the organisation from risk.

We have used the developing standard with boards as a discussion document to drive a strategic planning session around data use. We have spoken to boards, through think-tank sessions, who had experienced an embarrassing data incident and were keen to put governance in place to avoid a repeat event, and we have worked with boards who were keen to get into the 'data business' and didn't know where to start. Both types of audience found the standard very useful.

One of the directors we spoke to redesigned the delivery of his business based on our conversations, with real time monitoring of devices sited in very remote locations. Using Vodafone Narrowband and Microsoft Azure cloud services, we could create a service that would detect when the remote devices required maintenance or relocation, and we could deliver the service at a fraction of the previous cost for monitoring.

One of our data governance workshop attendees told us of issues with data exposed through a government agency. The data exposed was innocuous on its own, but when it was combined with other (freely available) data sets, it provided a register that would have greatly influenced the value of properties and other assets over a large area. The issue with government agencies and local and district councils providing open data sets is that it is difficult to withdraw them if any issues arise. The aim of most government bodies in releasing information is to enable entrepreneurial businesses to be built around the data. Withdrawing released data would most likely kill off the businesses grown up around it.

The standard can be used to prompt questions to be asked before data is collected or exposed, and to guide the development of strategy that will maximise value and minimise risk. However, even the best strategy in the world is useless without a solid implementation plan and supporting policies and controls.

Building a data strategy

Table 3.1 shows the table from Part 1 of the 38505 standard designed to assist a governing body or group of directors (a sub-committee of the board) in working through the development of a data strategy for their organisation. By the time the governing body has worked through the questions in each cell, they should have the basis for a data strategy and an idea of the data policies required for the strategy to be effective.

Table 3.1 Building a data strategy

	Value	Risk	Constraints
Collect	[V1] The governing body should decide the degree to which the organization will leverage or monetize data to achieve its strategic objectives.	[R1] The governing body should recognize the risks associated with the collection and use of data and agree to an acceptable level of their data risk within the overall risk appetite for the organization. This should include an examination of the risks of not collecting and using the data.	[C1] The governing body should approve the policies for data collection, taking into account constraints such as quality, privacy, consent requirements and transparency of use.
Store	[V2] The governing body should approve policies that allocate the appropriate resources for data storage and data subscription such that the potential value of data can be extracted.	[R2] The governing body should direct managers to ensure that an ISMS [information security management system] is in place extending to data and technology suppliers, with adequate resources, controls and trust such that the level of risk appetite is not exceeded.	[C2] The governing body should direct managers to ensure data storage practices (including third party data subscriptions) support the data collection constraints.

(Continued)

Table 3.1 (Continued)

	Value	Risk	Constraints
Report	[V3] The governing body should direct managers to use the necessary tools and technologies to ensure that the full value of data can be extracted.	[R3] The governing body should establish the significance of the context of data, including cultural norms, and its potential misinterpretation in aggregate.	[C3] The governing body should establish the importance of the relationship between data and its constraints, particularly if data is aggregated from different datasets.
Decide	[V4] The governing body should ensure that the data culture for the organization aligns with its data strategy including behaviours such as data access practices, data-enabled decision making and the organizational learning from the decision process.	[R4] The appropriate data and format should be delivered in a report for automated or human decision making. While remaining accountable for these decisions, the governing body should delegate decision making responsibilities appropriately for the organization and for the acceptable level of data risk.	[C4] The output of the decision making process, as new data, will have its own value, risk and constraints, and the governing body should set the expectations for the decision making process and associated responsibilities.
Distribute	[V5] The governing body should establish a policy for data distribution such that it allows the organization to satisfy the strategic plan of the organization.	[R5] The governing body should ensure that managers have implemented adequate controls to prevent inappropriate distribution.	[C5] The governing body should ensure that the appropriate distribution rights are implemented and that they are respected by third parties.
Dispose	[V6] The governing body should approve policies that allow for the disposal of data when the data is no longer valuable, or can no longer be held.	[R6] The governing body should direct managers to implement an appropriate data disposal process that includes such controls as the secure and permanent destruction of data.	[C6] The governing body should monitor data retention and disposal obligations and ensure that adequate processes have been implemented.

Note: Permission to reproduce extracts from ISO 38505 was granted by British Standards Institution (BSI). British Standards can be obtained in PDF or hard copy formats from the BSI online shop: www.bsigroup. com/Shop or by contacting BSI Customer Services for hardcopies only: Tel: +44 (0)20 8996 9001; email: cservices@bsigroup.com.

38505-2 IMPLEMENTING A DATA STRATEGY

Part 2 of the 38505 series, Information technology – Governance of IT – Governance of data – Part 2: Implications of ISO/IEC 38505-1 for data management, provides guidance on the implementation of a governance of data approach, starting with the deployment of a data strategy and following on from the theory of Part 1 (available at https://www.iso.org/standard/70911.html). Part 2 references the data accountability map and decision matrix from Part 1 and provides recommendations for the type of policy that should be developed to achieve the governance goals. It also suggests how these policies could be developed. Generally, a governing body would work in isolation to set strategy with associated goals and targets and to set policy to assist their management team with fulfilling the strategy. We have suggested an alternative approach for the implementation of data strategy. We recommend that policy is developed through close dialogue with the management team, to see what is currently possible and to identify what could be possible, subject to the provision of the required tools and resources. For example, let's consider the case where the management team has been tasked with developing a new data service. Putting together a data service is like assembling pieces for a jigsaw – in contrast to developing an application for a phone, which involves coding functions from scratch. The management team will most likely need assistance from somebody who has an idea what the finished jigsaw should look like, but they won't necessarily need to hire a team of developers. Policy should assist the management team in taking a good approach to the data service development, which could be different from their traditional approach to product development.

It is useful to note that your IT staff could feel threatened by your desire to deliver data-driven services. The smarter staff will adapt and work with you to provide new functions, but less visionary staff might be more protective of the empire that they have lovingly created and they might see data services as a threat to their livelihood. This could surface as 'significant security concerns' or 'significant costs', but the message that they are really trying to get across is 'does this mean you are replacing me?' This would be a good time to explain the difference between IT and data. Of course, if you are a taxi company switching entirely to an Uber model and you are planning on throwing out all your IT infrastructure, then your IT staff are correct to be concerned. It is more likely, though, that, if you are a taxi company that has already invested in IT infrastructure and taxis, you would be looking at introducing a data-driven service to make it easier for your customers to book a taxi, pay for a taxi and to see when the taxi is approaching.

In summary, if concerns are raised by the IT team, then take them seriously and investigate them. Don't take the concerns as gospel truth, but don't ignore them and do get assistance in responding to them if IT isn't your core capability. IT folk are very good at using acronyms to provide a smokescreen.

Developing data policy

Part 2 of the 38505 series of standards kicks off with a brief summary of Part 1. If you are considering investing in the ISO 38505 standards, we would recommend that you purchase all parts. Part 2 is very much a 'how to' guide, and without the background of Part 1, you might be left questioning why you are doing something. A third governance of data standard will provide insight into definitions and classifications relating to data, and will explain the use of terms across the series.

Part 2 takes the matrix of data accountability map points (*collect, store, report, decide, distribute* and *dispose*) and considerations (*value, risk, constraint*) and suggests questions to drive the development of policy. We see that the development of policy is an essential part of deploying a strategy and that deploying a strategy is the first key activity for introducing governance in a new area such as data. Policy is the contract between the governing body and the management team that ensures everybody knows what is expected of them in their particular role relating to the deployment of a new organisational strategic direction.

Creating policy for data is less straightforward than it might at first appear. There are two reasons for this. The first is that the approach to data is an area that is still maturing and changing. The second reason is that to provide a sound and sensible policy, directors need to understand the current capability and future potential of their organisation. This is best achieved through consultation with the management team and representatives from throughout the organisation.

Example policy statements and templates are provided in the standard. It is envisaged that some of the statements produced would be added on to existing organisational policies, and that some statements would be put together to create new policies. By the time you have worked through the standard, you should have policy to cover all aspects of data use throughout your organisation. There might be a tendency to attempt to 'boil the ocean' by some well-meaning participants, but a well facilitated discussion can pull the dreamers back to the reality of the core activities of the organisation and what the organisation is trying to achieve. Interestingly, working through the process with an organisation recently, it quickly split the room into conservatives and dreamers, but when the conservatives caught the vision of the dreamers, and the dreamers allowed themselves to be moderated by the conservatives, the result was a set of policy statements that stood the test of covering all aspects of data use.

Tables 3.2 and 3.3 show examples from the standard of guidance for developing policy relating to the *collect* activity.

Practical examples

Part 2 of the ISO governance of data 38505 standards ends with appendices that provide case study examples to demonstrate how the governance of data standards can be implemented.

To recap, we are assuming that the governing body or board of directors of an organisation has used Part 1 of the governance of data standards and worked through the questions in the considerations matrix to produce a data strategy, taking their first step on the governance of data journey. Having produced a data strategy, we encourage the governing body or board of directors to work through the policy considerations in Part 2 of the governance of data standards to co-develop policy that will enable the management team of the organisation to implement the data strategy.

Table 3.2 Collect considerations

	Value	Risk	Constraints
Collect considerations	Identify the value to be obtained from collecting data. This assists in determining the quality, quantity and sources of the data required.	Identify the risks associated with the collection of data such that the data strategy and the over-arching organizational strategy can be met.	Identify the constraints that apply to the types and sources of data to be collected. These constraints range from legislation and regulation to existing internal policy.
Policy	Once there is an understanding of the types and sources of data to be collected and the associated risks and constraints, a policy can be set to ensure that the collection of data throughout the organization meets the requirements of the data strategy.		
	This policy in turn can be used to determine appropriate measurements and reporting mechanisms to enable the governing body to monitor the delivery of the organizational data strategy.		

Table 3.3 Collect policy

	Value		Risk		Constraints
V1	**The governing body should decide the degree to which the organization will leverage or monetize data to achieve its strategic objectives.**	**R1**	**The governing body should recognize the risks associated with the collection and use of data and agree to an acceptable level of their data risk within the overall risk appetite for the organization. This should include an examination of the risks of not collecting and using the data.**	**C1**	**The governing body should approve the policies for data collection, taking into account constraints such as quality, privacy, consent requirements and transparency of use.**
Policy focus	The degree of being a 'data business'. *e.g.: Our focus is always on delivering a product that meets customer expectations including quality, timeliness and reliability of the service. Data use will support that goal.*		Acceptable level of data risk. The governing body decides the level of risk that the organization is prepared to take in order to achieve the strategic goals. *e.g.: We will only collect detailed data, such as location data or address, from our paying customers.*		*V1 + R1. Using the value/risk balance, the governing body sets the boundaries for the use of data. e.g.: Company policy will include the regulations of the regional markets, and in those regions, we will adopt the most restrictive requirements (e.g. in Western Europe we will default to German law unless otherwise stated).*
Data management options	Ways to collect data of value: • Buying/subscribing to data • Collecting Big Data • Internet of Things/sensors		Data collection risks and risk management considerations: • Quality of data collected ▪ Different data quality dimensions including completeness, consistency, uniqueness, validity and accuracy		Data collection constraints management considerations: • Privacy – notice and consent • Data use and transparency • Consolidating and updating personal information • Policy enforcement in email

(Continued)

Table 3.3 (Continued)

	Value	Risk	Constraints

	• 'Real time' data feeds (Really Simple Syndication (RSS), OData...)	• Input verification
		  ▪ Avoidance of input scripts
		  ▪ Man-in-the-middle attacks
		  ▪ Address validation
		  ▪ Fraud detection	

Monitoring performance and conformance	Ensuring valuable data is being collected: • Recording which data collections are being used for decision-making • Recording data-enabled decisions • Data classification	Ensuring data risk is managed: • Submitting responsibilities for approval • Submitting collection process for approval	Ensuring data constraints are being managed: • Allocating collecting resources • Making a list of regulation and legislation
Related standards		ISO 31000, on principles and guidelines for risk management; ISO TS 8000, on data quality; ISO TR 31004, on guidance for risk management.	ISO/IEC 29100, on privacy framework; ISO/IEC 19944, on data flow, data categories and data use.

The case studies provided in the standard are examples from the following sectors:

- travel;
- finance;
- transport.

The standards development committee was very grateful to the three contributing organisations who were generous in sharing their expertise.

The first of the four case studies is different from the rest, and relates to a purely fictional example created to assist with the development of the standard. It provided a double learning experience for the standards writers. First, the fictional scenario assisted with testing theories as to what needed to be written into the standard to provide useful guidance. Second, it provided a useful mechanism for developing new materials – a mechanism that I have used many times since!

Case study 1 – the fictional coffee shop

The first case study example in Part 2 of the governance of data standard concerns a fictional chain of coffee shops with branches in cities across China. As a group of standards writers, we role-played a board of directors implementing a data strategy for the *Example Coffee Shop* chain. We described the Example Coffee Shop as an enterprise planning to expand with stores in every major town and city, wanting to drive closer connections with customers and to build data-driven services to encourage customer loyalty.

Who were our customers? What was it our customers wanted, apart from a good quality cup of coffee? Were they concerned about Fair Trade and where their coffee beans came from? Were they annoyed at having to queue for coffee and did they want the option of ordering ahead? Could we implement smarter stock control and supply centred around our customers' needs, the weather, travel conditions? Could the shops 'learn' from each other? What benefits could we provide for our customers once we knew their ordering habits and likes and dislikes? If we started storing data on our customers, what permissions did we need from them? How could we use this data to build a new range of coffees or expand to other drinks?

As a group of fictional directors, we had a very lively discussion around our fictional new company. Having set our goals and vision for our organisation, we worked through the matrix of questions and considerations at the end of Part 1 of the 38505 series and developed our data strategy to govern how we would use data across all our stores. Having appointed a CEO, we then worked with the CEO, using the guidance from Part 2, to develop policy statements. We had a very productive discussion and the more we discussed policy, the more we realised what we could do with collected data. The more we discussed the use of the data, the more we recognised the need for clear policy and boundaries. For example, we imagined that our coffee shops provided free Wi-Fi for customers, and we envisaged that our fictional stores would have camera surveillance for protecting the staff in the shop. We had the technology in place to photo the queue and to provide photos through our website so that customers could wait for the queue to die down before rushing across to order. We thought it would be very likely that our customers would find observing the queue from their offices and desks a very useful feature. However, we recognised that we couldn't show a camera feed without the express permission of individuals, and that we might put potential customers off if we asked everybody entering a store to sign a consent for data use form.

The Example Coffee Shop demonstrated to us the value of enabling a data policy discussion between the governing body and the executive management team. It showed how such a conversation would develop an evolving picture of what an organisation could offer by implementing data-enabled services, and how each new service could trigger a number of policy questions that would have to be answered by the governing body before the management team could proceed with implementation.

Even though our group example was fully fictional, we were able to work through the guidance in the 38505 standards and highlight issues and concerns that would need to be addressed, and identify policy that would need to be put in place. We noted that most of our policy statements would have been additions to existing organisational policy, and we would not have been generating many new policy documents. Once policy had been identified, we needed to work out how we would monitor the delivery of our data strategy. How would we know which of our new services was the most profitable or worthwhile? How could we measure customer loyalty and returning customers? How could we check for breaches of our security and privacy policies? Would we know if our data had been hacked? How could we encourage our customers to be data- and data security-savvy without putting arduous demands on them? Monitoring is a key element of governance, and especially vital when introducing new services.

By the end of our fictional exercise we were confident that we had identified the policy to help us meet the goals of our data strategy and, through that, to meet our organisational goals.

More importantly, as a group of standards writers, we were able to test, check, tweak and add to the guidance in Part 2 of the standard from our role-play experience.

A fictional example is all well and good, and it did help us immensely in checking our own development work. However, there is nothing to compare with a real-life example, and the second appendix of the standard has exactly that.

Case study 2 – travel service company
The second example in the standard shows the data governance policies put in place by a large travel company with a comprehensive range of services, and the thinking behind the development of their governance structure. The travel company referenced specialises in bespoke luxury travel experiences, and successfully matching itineraries to customers based on customer age, interests, work and other activities. This case study provides a good example of using data analysis to continually learn and evaluate what sort of people would be interested in specific travel experiences, so that the organisation can make recommendations that are taken up by customers and enjoyed. Feedback from their customers has been very positive.

Case study 3 – Chinese financial industry
The third case study example published in the standard has been provided by the Chinese Securities Commission to demonstrate the data policies and management tools in place to control the large volume of high-quality transactional data that daily flows

through the Chinese Stock Exchange. This case study demonstrates the governance controls that are required when processing large quantities of data where accuracy and timeliness are vital components in supporting reliable and trustworthy market analysis.

Case study 4 – air transport IT company

The fourth example was provided by an infrastructure company based in Europe managing global communications and providing services for airline commercial management to airports based in over 200 countries and territories. In pre-COVID-19 years, they provided the systems that checked in over a billion airline passengers per year. They use the data strategy developed using Part 1 of the 38505 standard to:

> identify the strategic value, risk and constraints presented by different types of data flowing through its systems and thus determine how such data aligns with its core mission and strategy.
>
> (ISO/IEC 38505-2 Governance of data standard Part 2)

SUMMARY

The ISO 38505 series of governance of data standards provide guidance for the development of a data governance framework for an organisation. The standards are centred around a data accountability map that identifies the areas in an organisation where data governance needs to be applied.

Using the data accountability map, Part 1 of the 38505 series of standards guides organisations through the development of a data strategy and decision-making model that takes into account the value, risks and constraints of data use and aligns data-related decisions with the intended direction of the organisation.

Part 2 of the 38505 series of standards covers the creation of data policy to guide the deployment of the data strategy across the organisation to realise the full value of data use as identified in the setting of the data strategy. Part 2 of the standard also includes case studies from organisations that have used Part 1 to develop their data strategy, to demonstrate the theory of data governance in practice.

One of the most significant challenges of data governance in practice is connectedness, and the next chapter will look at this challenge in further detail.

4   GOVERNING DATA: DEALING WITH CONNECTIVITY

Alisdair McKenzie

One of the key requirements of a governing body in the 21st century is to protect organisational data and information through directing good information security practice. Developing a data strategy and the associated data policy to deliver to an organisational vision and mission are the first steps on the data governance journey. Once a data-enabled service or product is in place, information security is a key consideration. Can the service be hacked or compromised? Does this situation get more complicated to monitor if the data-enabled service is part of an IoT delivery?

This chapter presents examples of security incidents and issues in IoT applications, identifying their causes and the security best practices that could have reduced their impact. It demonstrates the complexity of governing data in a connected world.

Analysis of the small sample of these examples shows the common issues that arise and, for some, what can and has been done to improve security performance. Where available, this chapter will identify sanctions applied to the enterprises responsible for the affected systems. It will also review elements of guidance issued by government and industry for good practice in the development of IoT applications and systems. Through the analysis of selected case studies involving security breaches, this chapter will demonstrate the value of good data governance when operating with multiple connected systems or when collecting data from multiple sensors or devices – such as in an IoT deployment.

ISSUES WITH A CONNECTED WORLD

The relentless advance of a 'connected world' has led to exponential growth of the volumes and variety of data generated by enterprises as they go about their business, be they governmental, for-profit (private sector) or not-for-profit.

This data is essential to the business and takes a number of forms, such as business plans, proprietary knowledge, trade secrets, financial data, trading data, customer data, personal information about clients and so on.

Take this example: in the analogue era there were 12 data points about annual energy consumption at my house (six actual bimonthly readings and six inter-reading estimates).

> With a digital smart meter recording minute by minute, there are now 525,600 data points, allowing a precise profile of consumption to be shown. This also provides an opportunity to construct a multifaceted profile of the activities at my house if one has access to this data.
>
> Do I 'own' my data? Apparently not. When I look at the terms and conditions document that I accepted back in the analogue era, I find: 'You agree that we own all meter reading information.'

This trove of data requires varying levels of protection, depending on its nature and its value, real and perceived, to a number of parties within or outside the enterprise's environment.

The situation is further complicated by the fact that no application stands alone but instead operates within a complex chain (communications infrastructure, embedded devices, third-party services, operating systems, application programs, end point devices, etc) (Roberts 2014). The enterprise will be dependent on the elements of the chain to deliver its service, but will not be directly in control of most of them. Additionally, this complexity leads to a blurring in the ownership of the data and where the custodial and stewardship responsibilities fall.

The governing body of an enterprise must be aware of the large number of issues this complexity and huge volume of data brings and what they must do to ensure that this data is adequately governed and protected while in their enterprise.

What has happened so far?

Historically, many governments and regulators have been slow in providing guidance and regulation to support governors of enterprises in discharging their duties in respect of the governance of data.

There have been a number of significant breaches of data security/privacy in recent years. The UK Information Commissioner's Office was an early starter in penalising the misuse of data by law enforcement authorities. In 2013 the Commissioner ruled that the use of automatic number plate recognition (ANPR) cameras in the town of Royston to capture car registration data was excessive and unlawful. The Information Commissioner's Office head of enforcement, Stephen Eckersley, said:

> It is difficult to see why a small rural town such as Royston requires cameras monitoring all traffic in and out of the town 24 hours a day. The use of ANPR cameras and other forms of surveillance must be proportionate to the problem it is trying to address. After detailed enquiries, including consideration of the information Hertfordshire Constabulary provided, we found that this simply wasn't the case in Royston.
>
> (Fiveash 2013)

A 2014 study of IoT devices by HP shows that many devices and applications used in the smart home and by individuals have also been found to have serious security shortcomings (HP 2014). The HP press release describes the specifics of the common security shortcomings identified and how they can be mitigated. Many can be rectified by implementing known good practice.

Examples of these breaches will be discussed later in this chapter. Thankfully there is now a wide range of guidance documents becoming available for developers at all levels, from governors and management to technical practitioners. Regulations are emerging and evolving as regulators address the challenges of ensuring the safe and reasonable use of data-enabled devices. For example, the UK Drone and Model Aircraft Code is continually modified as new risks and opportunities arise (CAA 2021). Following drone disruption to flights at Gatwick Airport, it was updated in March 2019 to restrict flying close to airfields, and was updated again on 31 December 2020 to align with European Aviation Safety Agency guidance.

As stated at the start of this chapter, many data-enabled services and products become part of an IoT delivery. When introducing governance of data for an organisation, the governing body needs to work through the risk and security considerations associated with the use of their data service or product in the context of interactions with other data-enabled services and products.

A 2019 publication from the EU's European Telecommunications Standards Institute (ETSI), 'Cyber security for consumer Internet of Things' (ETSI 2019) provides 13 cybersecurity provisions, which are identical to the 'Code of practice for consumer IoT security' issued by the UK government in October 2018 (DCMS 2018a).

This code of practice applies to consumer IoT products that are connected to the internet and/or home network and associated services. A non-exhaustive list of examples includes:

- Connected children's toys and baby monitors,
- Connected safety-relevant products such as smoke detectors and door locks,
- Smart cameras, TVs and speakers,
- Wearable health trackers,
- Connected home automation and alarm systems,
- Connected appliances (e.g. washing machines, fridges),
- Smart home assistants.

Another useful document from the UK Department for Digital, Culture, Media & Sport is 'Mapping of IoT security recommendations, guidance and standards to the UK's code of practice for consumer IoT security' (DCMS 2018b), which contains mappings to some 58 guidance documents detailing standards, frameworks, best practices and so on. The document includes advice from various entities, such as governments, industry associations, professional bodies, practitioner societies and vendors.

The following examples show where a lack of good governance of data can lead to security vulnerabilities in the areas of:

- automobiles;
- connected medical devices;
- smart homes;
- business practice data protection.

The examples demonstrate that when an organisation moves from the manufacture of a traditional product (a car, a medical device, a house, a camera) to a data-enabled version of a traditional product (a driverless car, a pacemaker that can be remotely updated, a smart home, an internet-connected camera), then there is a requirement for the governing body to understand the new risk, value and compliance profile for the new product. Faults and errors resulting from a failure to address the issues brought by a rapid move to data services and products can be attributed to poor data governance practices.

Automobiles

In August 2014 researchers Charlie Miller and Chris Valasek presented their paper, 'A survey of remote automotive attack surfaces', at the Black Hat security conference, USA (Miller and Valasek n.d.). At that time they concluded that, while it's possible to remotely access – and in some cases, take limited control – of a vehicle, the process was difficult in practice and very much depended on the model targeted.

This research found a wide variety of vulnerabilities across the cars tested, and ranked the models from low to high vulnerability. A major concern was the lack of segregation of computer functions within an unsegregated architecture. Only one model had an IT architecture that separated safety critical functions from entertainment.

At the companion DefCon later in August 2014, a group of concerned security researchers, 'I Am The Cavalry', released a '5 Star Automotive Cyber Safety Program', which encouraged manufacturers to improve the quality of the computer security as implemented in their vehicles (Leyden 2014).

One year later, in July 2015, Miller and Valesek demonstrated remote takeover of a vehicle out on the road from 10 miles away via the internet (Greenberg 2015). This demonstrated that the current generation of vehicles still contained many vulnerabilities and would not be able to protect their occupants against a sustained, competent attack.

In 2015 automotive manufacturers from North America, Europe and Asia committed to set up 'Auto-ISAC' (Automotive Information Sharing and Analysis Center). This organisation issued a 'best practices' document in July 2016 (Auto-ISAC 2016). These best practices frequently reference the National Institute of Standards and Technology (NIST), the Society of Automobile Engineers and ISO/IEC standards for guidance, and support sector-wide data governance to avoid unintended outcomes from uncontrolled, unauthorised data sharing.

Connected medical devices

In 2012, the television series *Homeland* depicted the assassination of Vice President Walden by the remote manipulation of his implantable cardioverter device (ICD) pacemaker (season 2, episode 10, 'Broken Hearts'). This is a fictional example demonstrating that poor data governance can result in unintended data sharing with fatal consequences.

The scenario was initially characterised as fanciful; however, it was later revealed to be based on an actual security concern. In 2001, US Vice President Dick Cheney's medical advisors bought his original ICD anonymously and sealed it before announcing the pending operation. In 2007, when the ICD required replacement due to battery expiry, they requested a special order custom device without wireless adjustment capability, which by then came as standard. The replacement device had many more features than its predecessor, including data collection of a number of elements and download capability (Cheney et al. 2014). Cheney said of the assassination plot from the award-winning series:

> I found [the depiction] credible because I knew from the experience we had and the necessity for adjusting my own device, that it was an accurate portrayal of what was possible.
>
> (Fenner 2013)

Indeed, for a number of years security researchers have identified security vulnerabilities in high-tech medical devices such as insulin pumps and IV dripmeters as well as ICD pacemakers (Wadhwa and Wadhwa 2012).

In January 2016 the security researcher group 'I Am The Cavalry' proposed a 'Hippocratic oath for connected medical devices' (I Am The Cavalry 2016). The group were also participants in the US Food and Drug Administration (FDA) public workshop on 'Collaborative approaches to medical device cybersecurity' held 20–21 January 2016 (FDA 2016a).

The connected medical device spectrum is more complex than that of automobiles, with a larger range of suppliers and participants. It is therefore a more difficult task to bring common standards and robust governance practices to the field.

Further US FDA guidance for addressing security issues with connected medical devices is identified later in this chapter.

Smart homes

The 21st century is seeing the concept of the 'smart home' becoming a reality. Current technology allows us to connect our domestic appliances, heating, ventilation and air conditioning, lamps, doors, cameras and home entertainment together via the internet with the promise that we can control our environment and life from anywhere on the planet. These are widespread instances of the IoT. They require the connection of many elements of hardware, software, operating systems, infrastructure services, communications protocols and so on in a complex chain – and the complexity of this chain means there are many places where things can go wrong.

The HP report discussed earlier identified common shortcomings in IoT applications in the smart home and personal use. The TRENDnet example discussed below is another example of an inadequately secured smart home application.

While the benefits promised are manifold, the reality is that, to date, the treatment of the risks that this concept brings has been woefully inadequate in many instances; the implementation of many smart home applications has been flawed in a number of prominent cases. It has since become more recognised that a governing body should be responsible for following good data practices and providing protection for those who use or consume their products and services. Ignorance of the consequences of poor data practices is not an acceptable excuse.

Business practice data protection

The US Federal Trade Commission (FTC) has used existing law to obtain settlements from enterprises it has alleged were not providing adequate protection for individuals' data in their business practices. These settlements required the enterprises to cease their deceptive practices, submit to a programme of independent audit and pay monetary penalties. This situation should encourage members of governance boards to require their management to ensure that adequate data protection and security practices are followed. Two examples of FTC action follow.

TRENDnet security cameras
Early in 2012, a security blogger reported a security vulnerability in some models of TRENDnet security cameras connected to the internet (Leyden 2012). Basically, the flaw allowed video output from the cameras to be accessed by anyone who could identify the internet address of the camera – a fairly trivial task for anyone with basic IT technical knowledge.

TRENDnet had been selling around US$6 million worth of the cameras per year since 2010 (approximately 10 per cent of its revenue). The cameras were used for a wide variety of purposes, including monitoring baby nurseries and other private domestic rooms. A product feature was that they allowed remote visual and audio access to the data using vendor-supplied application software. TRENDnet's marketing and product information described the product as 'secure' in several places. The FTC complaint alleged that these claims that the cameras were secure was unfounded and that the faulty software left the data streams exposed:

> TRENDnet is prohibited from misrepresenting the security of its cameras or the security, privacy, confidentiality, or integrity of the information that its cameras or other devices transmit. In addition, the company is barred from misrepresenting the extent to which a consumer can control the security of information the cameras or other devices store, capture, access, or transmit.
>
> (FTC 2014a)

> TRENDnet also is required to establish a comprehensive information security program designed to address security risks that could result in unauthorized access to or use of the company's devices, and to protect the security, confidentiality, and integrity of information that is stored, captured, accessed, or transmitted by its devices. The company also is required to obtain third-party assessments of its security programs every two years for the next 20 years.
>
> (FTC 2014b)

TRENDnet were also required by the FTC to notify customers about the security issues and the software fixes available, and to provide free technical support for customers for the next two years to assist with updating and/or uninstalling their cameras.

Path social networking application
The Path social networking application collected user personal data without the users' consent, even if the user had not selected a permissive option (FTC 2013). The FTC press release, dated 1 February 2013, states that:

> Path operates a social networking service that allows users to keep journals about "moments" in their life and to share that journal with a network of up to 150 friends. Through the Path app, users can upload, store, and share photos, written "thoughts," the user's location, and the names of songs to which the user is listening.

The issue of concern to the FTC was that the Path app collected and stored personal contacts even if the user had not selected the option 'Find friends from your contacts'. This personal contact information included first and last names, addresses, phone numbers, email addresses, Facebook and Twitter usernames and dates of birth.

In February 2013 the FTC settled a complaint alleging that Path deceived consumers and improperly collected personal information from users' mobile address books. The settlement required Path Inc. to establish a comprehensive privacy programme and to obtain independent privacy assessments every other year for the next 20 years. The company also paid $800,000 to settle charges that it illegally collected personal information from children without their parents' consent.

ADDRESSING ISSUES OF THE CONNECTED WORLD

Progress is being made to address these issues with the connected world, and there is a growing body of guidance in the form of standards and papers available to provide advice for a governing body making the change from a traditional product to a data-enabled product.

In addition to the broad standards from UK and the EU already identified, the US Underwriters Laboratories has developed UL 2900-1 ANSI/CAN/UL Standard for Software Cybersecurity for Network-Connectable Products. This includes the Cybersecurity Assurance Program (CAP) that has been adopted by the US FDA for guidance on security for connected medical devices (UL 2017).

Automotive

Automotive industry developments such as the Auto-ISAC suggest that manufacturers are beginning to both become aware of their duty of care and take responsibility for the safety of their products. This will go some way to protect the people who use these new data-enabled products.

Underwriters Laboratories has drafted UL 4600, a safety standard governing self-driving cars. Formation of an advisory panel comprising a diverse group of stakeholders is underway to guide ongoing revisions to the standard and achieve its publication (UL n.d.).

Medical devices

The US FDA has issued two guidance documents in regard to cybersecurity for medical devices (FDA 2014, 2016b), with acknowledgement of the fact that many such devices are now connected to networks including the internet and are capable of being remotely accessed. These documents identify requirements for managing the security of medical devices. When addressing governance of data, governing bodies should require their enterprise managers to consider reviewing such advice as part of good practice.

The first document (FDA 2014) covers the design and development of medical devices, and the second (FDA 2016b) emphasises that manufacturers should monitor, identify and address cybersecurity vulnerabilities and exploits as part of their post-market management of medical devices.

Smart homes

As mentioned earlier, after a slow start there are a wide range of guidance documents becoming available for developers at all levels.

IoT applications in smart homes use data that affects all aspects of life, including health, safety, privacy, security, finance and convenience. The EU ETSI and UK standards and guidance, identified earlier in this chapter, provide a good foundation for enterprises creating safe and secure applications and systems in this wide-ranging field.

Business practice data protection

Guidance for businesses sharing personal data comes through multiple sources, including privacy legislation, health and safety providers, financial institutions and entertainment creators.

Governing body members should ensure that the IoT applications and systems they commission are developed using security good practice and with regard to current available standards and guidelines. In addition to standards and guidance from the UK, US and EU governments already discussed, there are also open source alternatives, such as OWASP.

OWASP – Open Web Application Security Project
OWASP is a non-profit foundation that works to improve the security of software. It oversees an OWASP Internet of Things Project to address security issues in IoT systems and applications. It also manages a project to provide an application security verification standard.

OWASP Internet of Things Project
The OWASP Internet of Things Project is designed to help manufacturers, developers and consumers better understand the security issues associated with the IoT, and to enable users in any context to make better security decisions when building, deploying or assessing IoT technologies.

OWASP Application Security Verification Standard
The OWASP Application Security Verification Standard Project provides a basis for testing web application technical security controls and also provides developers with a list of requirements for secure development.

SUMMARY

As the IoT continues to gather speed, enabling disparate data sets and systems to be joined in ways that have not been possible previously, there is an increasing need to consider the governance of data beyond the boundaries of an organisation and to consider the consequences (from a security viewpoint, in particular) when opening up or joining new data services.

Good data governance practices can assist with compliance, such as alignment with privacy legislation, limitation of risk to adverse incidents and reduction in liability for adverse consequences, and can protect individuals from the negative, unintended consequences of data sharing.

FURTHER READING

The following books, papers and articles provide predictions around the use and misuse of IoT networks, which will become ubiquitous as 5G networks are deployed around the world. These 5G networks are enablers for rapid, many-point to many-point data sharing and introduce a new level of complexity for governing data.

Anderson, R. (2015) The internet of bad things, observed. Presentation to VB2015, Prague, September 2015. Virus Bulletin. https://www.virusbulletin.com/uploads/pdf/conference_slides/2015/Anderson-VB2015.pdf.

Da Costa, F. (2013) *Rethinking the Internet of Things*. Apress Media.

Dhanjani, N. (2015) *Abusing the Internet of Things*. O'Reilly.

Greengard, S. (2015) *The Internet of Things*. MIT Press

Ohlhausen, M. (2013) The Internet of Things and the FTC: Does innovation require intervention? Federal Trade Commission, 18 October. https://www.ftc.gov/public-statements/2013/10/internet-things-ftc-does-innovation-require-intervention.

Ohlhausen, M. (2013) Remarks of Commissioner Maureen K. Ohlhausen, FTC Internet of Things workshop. The Internet of Things: When things talk among themselves. Federal Trade Commission, 19 December. https://www.ftc.gov/public-statements/2013/11/remarks-commissioner-maureen-k-ohlhausen-ftc-internet-things-workshop.

Roberts, P (2015) Video: Ross Anderson on the Internet of Bad Things. *the security ledger*, 13 November. https://securityledger.com/2015/11/video-ross-anderson-on-the-internet-of-bad-things/.

Schneier, B. (2015) *Data and Goliath: The Hidden Battles to Collect Your Data and Control Your World*. W. W. Norton & Co.

Schneier, B. (2016) Real-world security and the Internet of Things. *Schneier on Security*, 28 July. https://www.schneier.com/blog/archives/2016/07/real-world_secu.html.

Schneier, B. (2018) *Click Here to Kill Everybody: Security and Survival in a Hyper-connected World*. W. W. Norton & Co.

PART 2
DATA ACCOUNTABILITY

Part 2 of the book takes a deeper look at the data accountability map from the ISO 38505 standards, outlined in Part 1, and the individual data functions of *collect*, *store*, *decide*, *report*, *distribute* and *dispose*. Each chapter is written by a different author, who describes their application of the data accountability map in the context of their work and cultural experience. The authors come from around the world, together bringing views from Europe, Asia, Australasia and the Americas.

QUICK RECAP

The centrepiece for the ISO theory of 'governing data' is the data accountability map, as shown in Figure P2.1. The ISO 38505 series of standards for the governance of data provides guidelines for developing a governance framework and for implementing the policy required to ensure that the framework is put into practice, influencing all data-related decisions across the organisation. The data accountability map identifies six areas where governance considerations must be applied. These areas are where data is collected and stored, how data is used for decision making and for reporting, and how data is eventually distributed and disposed. At each area, the governing body is encouraged to apply the three considerations of value, risk and constraint. Following these guidelines will ensure that data is used to the best advantage across the organisation, while not exposing the organisation to unnecessary risk or breaking the constraints of legislation and internal policy.

DATA ACCOUNTABILITY MAP POINTS

In the following chapters, each author takes one of the data accountability map points and applies their personal experience and insight in delivering governance solutions. As you will see from the short author biographies listed at the front of this book, this experience comes from a range of industrial, governmental and academic areas.

Data does not pass through border Customs or enter into quarantine as it passes across national boundaries, and yet we still see many organisations carrying out business with a national view of their data. These next six chapters will open up some different approaches to governance of data, taken from geographically dispersed subject matter experts.

Figure P2.1 Data accountability map

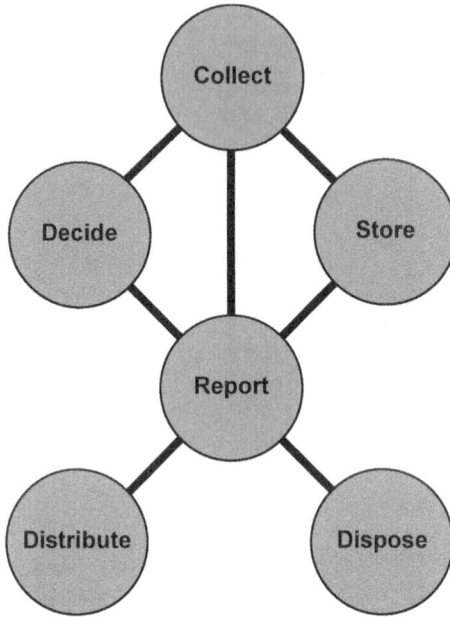

5   COLLECT

Li Ming and Rose Pan

Data collection is the first procedure of data accountability introduced in ISO/IEC 38505-1, which is the application of ISO/IEC 38500 (the ISO Governance of IT standard) to the governance of data.

The governing body should consider the value, risk and constraints relating to data collection for their business. They should formulate strategies and policy about data collection, and realise that value, risk and constraints are the important aspects of data collection. These aspects interact with each other, as data value will be achieved by risk reduction and constraint satisfaction. They should be considered in detail and in depth to improve understanding for the governing body.

Figure 5.1 Governance of data collection

Collection		
Value	Risk	Constraints
Customer requirement	Risk appetite	Privacy & conformance
Business strategy	Scope & method	Laws & regulations
Responsibility & accountability	Align with risk profile	Tools & expense
Culture	Role & responsibility	Capability of staff
Quality	Information security	Investment

VALUE

For the aspect of value related to data collection, the governing body should consider how to effectively collect data to meet the business requirements of the organisation. A precursor to this consideration is a check to ensure that all data currently being collected has been identified as necessary for collection.

The data to be collected will depend upon the part of the organisation requesting the data: human resources seeking information to align salaries; customer services looking for data relating to product use and customer satisfaction; research looking for data regarding market trends.

The governing body needs to define a business strategy and to be able to identify and find customers/users, and these activities need to be supported by a data strategy, including strategy for data collection. The governing body should also consider marketing requirements and the types of data that should be collected to support these activities.

Thus, the governing body needs to consider data collection as part of the overall business and data strategy and to set the direction for the performance of data analysis by the management body. The governing body should also realise that data collection is a professional and technical process, and that the management body will need sufficient resources and tools to enable the processes of data collection. The governing body should define the responsibility and accountability for data collection, and direct the management body to formulate seamless, expert data collecting processes. There is also a requirement for the governing body to design a mechanism to evaluate the results and processes of data collection.

Innovative culture can be encouraged by the governing body through the empowerment of the management body to create new methodology and technology for data collecting processes.

Data quality is an important consideration that should be covered by the strategy of data collection, since it is the prerequisite of fit-for-purpose data utilities. Poor-quality data increases the cost and time to produce outcomes, so the governing body should explicitly direct the development of data quality policy, direct the classification of data and direct the development of internal data practices to normalise the processes and results of data collection.

Data quality is improved by using commonly understood terms and by defining a standard around key terms. If two government agencies collect name information and one agency collects using the term 'official name' and the other uses the term 'name', they could pick up two different values from the same person. For example, a person whose official name was James might enter Jim for name. When these two agencies come to share information or use their collected data to verify identity, this becomes an issue. A common data collection standard across all government agencies would resolve this issue. In 2016, a man known to the New Zealand prison service as 'Phillip John Smith' fled to Brazil while on temporary release from Spring Hill Prison, using a passport bearing his birth name (and official name) 'Phillip John Traynor'.

(Meng-Yee 2016)

RISK

For the aspect of risks associated with data collection, potential risks should be considered carefully because risk may significantly impact the results and processes of data collection. For example, incorrect data collecting processes could bring the risk of data errors, and data collection from multiple sources may result in data inconsistencies. Thus, the governing body should design the risk appetite of data according to the risk appetite of the enterprise, and specify clearly the scope and method of data collection to reduce the risks associated with it. Furthermore, the governing body should also formulate targets for data quality and data integrity and direct the development of policy for data risk management in alignment with enterprise risk profiles. Roles and responsibilities for data collection need to be clearly assigned.

Also, the governing body should approve and monitor a procedure of risk identification, analysis, assessment and disposition of data for the avoidance of unauthorised data collection. Information security is the main risk associated with data, and the governing body should consider it an important issue. They should direct the establishment of a suitable information security framework through identification of the information security risks associated with the processes of data collection, for example data leakage by internal staff, data loss over an unencrypted transfer, collecting infected data and so on. The governing body should direct the management body to establish an information security management mechanism to identify information security risk points, to formulate a risk control matrix and to define the necessary procedures to control risks relating to data collection.

Information security risk is a factor at each point of the data accountability map.

CONSTRAINTS

For the aspect of constraints relating to data collection, the governing body should understand very clearly that data collection from outside the enterprise requires a consideration of data privacy and conformance. For example, many regions in China specify that the data of underage children should not be collected for any business purposes. Such constraints affect the process for data collection. The governing body is required to understand the external environment of the enterprise, including the local laws and regulations and industry standards relating to their business, so that they can define policies required for compliance and the framework required to monitor compliance. For example, a disclaimer relating to how collected data will be used by an enterprise should be drafted in compliance with local regulation, and in a manner acceptable to both the enterprise and the individual or organisation that the data is being collected from.

Another possible constraint of data collection is that the processes of data collection could require advanced tools at great cost to the enterprise. The governing body should also seek clarification that internal resources can support the proposed processes for data collection. If so, they should formulate the strategy and policies of data collection according to the existing resources, the level of technology available and the capability of staff, otherwise the enterprise will not achieve targets relating to data collection, since the expected value would be reduced by the investment in additional resources. If the governing body decides to approve investment in new tools or platforms for data collection, and to increase the training for related staff to increase their capability, then the governing body should set in place mechanisms to monitor and evaluate the investment for data collection continuously for maximum data value.

As part of their role in being accountable for data collection across the enterprise, the governing body should also apply the EDM model introduced in ISO/IEC 38500. They should formulate the strategy and policy for data collection, monitor the conformance and performance according to the control procedure during data collection, and evaluate the technology and capability based on the plan and proposal made by the management body.

> The consideration of data collection is related to the other governance of data accountabilities: *store*, *report*, *decide*, *distribute* and *dispose*. Aspects of data collection should also be considered when developing policy relating to the other accountabilities. For example, data quality, data security and data privacy should be considered as global issues across the whole framework in the development of a robust data strategy.

DATA COLLECTION: CASE STUDY

There are two main distinct approaches to enterprise data collection. The first approach is to collect as much data as possible that is associated with the enterprise, and to integrate it into one platform. The second approach is business-oriented and focuses on collecting data to meet specific demands. It requires less investment than the first approach, but it is less likely to support an innovative business searching for new products and services. These two different approaches result in different data strategies, policies, management processes and controls.

AA company is an online business-to-consumer trading platform and its board chair declares that 'their future relies on data'. Their product is data itself. All their business is online business, with a range of data collection sources: some data coming from user registrations; some from browsers; some from PCs; some from mobile phones and IoT equipment; and some from external partners. Their strategy is to collect as much data as possible, but there is no consistency in terms of data collection due to the complexity of the formats from the different input sources.

BB company is an education service organisation providing books and CDs via a mail catalogue to parents. They provide early childhood products by age and specific themes and they have more than one million users in China. The information collected by the company includes: the names of parents and children; the birth dates of children; home addresses; phone numbers and so on. BB company provides not only published materials for sale, but also the opportunity for children to participate in activities. Their policy is to protect users' privacy, the strategy is to provide an education service and the mission is to support children's potential development.

The following is the company's policy and the associated controls relating to data collection:

> When the company engages in on-site activities or provides gift samples online, it requires each user to fill out his/her name, email address, phone number and other contact information. Independent of activity, as long as the user's information is collected, there will be a statement provided to limit usage of the information to develop BB company's future activities and product development.

COMPARISON OF THE TWO CASES

Company AA and company BB operate with very different governance policies, and both are fit for purpose for the types of business that they operate in. One is an organisation collecting lots of data and looking for patterns from that data (company AA); the other organisation is collecting precise and accurate data to be able to provide a highly customised service (company BB).

This short example demonstrates that the optimum framework for data governance will be different for different organisations, organisational structures and business models.

Table 5.1 Comparison of two companies

	AA company	BB company
Company strategy regarding data	Their future is reliant on data. Data is their core business.	Their core competence is children's educational product development, and keeping the confidentiality of their client and partner information is core to their business.
Collection policy	Collect as much as possible.	Collect as needed, with the promise that the information will not be used without the permission of the provider.
Storage policy	Big Data platform with good management regarding cost and quality.	Encrypted sensitive data protected in a virtual environment.
Reporting and distribution	Reporting is not only used by AA, but also sold to their customers. They encourage feedback on data, with the aim of creating a data ecosystem with continuous inputs and outputs.	BB control access to reports and do not share client data directly with third parties.

SUMMARY

An organisation's approach to data governance for the collection of data will depend very much on the type of business, the organisational structure and the business model adopted. There is no 'one size fits all' approach to setting guidelines to govern how data should be collected. The 38505 series of standards can assist by encouraging an organisation to consider the risk, value and constraints associated with data collection and to determine data policy for collection that ensures the volume, quality and type of data collected and the frequency of data collection are fit for purpose.

6 STORE

Beenish Saeed

The data accountability map reflects on the *store* activity, which can include anything from locating data in a place of physical or logical retrieval, to data stored on devices within organisations as well as external to organisations. This also includes virtual stores such as data feeds. Whether an organisation is putting data to work, such as a hotel using data on their guests' clothing behaviours to improve their hotel laundry processes, or a business intelligence company doing a data inventory, it is important to ensure that governance policies are in place and accountabilities can be met.

ISO/IEC 38505-1 examines the data-specific aspects of *store*, noting that the value, risks and constraints associated with particular data sets will vary over time, so the onus is on the governing body to determine an appropriate review cycle for their organisation.

The standard presents questions to be considered when examining data-specific aspects of value, risk and constraints associated with *store* in order to develop a governance framework. Whether it is a corporate arm of a retail giant seeking to store customer data or an investment bank trying to inform clients to short-sell a stock, governing bodies and organisations must develop a governance framework that leverages the maximum value of data within their data risk appetite and takes into account internal and external constraints.

This chapter will combine the considerations from the governance of data standard (38505) with the principles of the overarching governance of IT standard (38500) to provide some insight into data storage matters of relevance to a governing body.

APPLYING THE PRINCIPLES OF GOVERNANCE

The six principles of governance listed in ISO/IEC 38500 are extended by the governance of data model in ISO/IEC 38505-1 to guide governing bodies and organisations in making decisions for the data accountability point of *store*. These six principles are:

- Principle 1 – responsibility;
- Principle 2 – strategy;
- Principle 3 – acquisition;
- Principle 4 – performance;
- Principle 5 – conformance;
- Principle 6 – human behaviour.

Principle 1: responsibility

When setting out responsibility in relation to data storage, it's important to ensure that relevant job responsibilities are understood and accepted, and those with responsibility for actions relating to demand for and supply of data have the authority to perform those actions. The principle goes further to stress the responsibility of governing bodies to also evaluate the competence of database administrators who assist business managers.

Following this, there must be a system to regularly monitor the appropriate mechanisms for data governance and the performance of those given responsibility in the governance of IT in line with the data culture.

This will help organisations in leveraging and protecting their data along with building a coherent governance framework. A clear organisational view of what is expected from managers and from staff may also result in the increased retention of business managers at executive and management levels.

> According to the Forbes Insights Team, a CDO's average tenure is just 2.4 years.
> (Insights Team 2019)

With a robust data strategy that clarifies the types and purpose of data and responsibility around its storage, managerial decision making can be better supported with a superior model of data governance.

Principle 2: strategy

The principle of strategy advises governing bodies to ensure that plans and policies, in this case around data use and storage, align with the organisation's objectives and satisfy key legitimate stakeholder requirements. In evaluating a strategy, governing bodies must also ensure that data use is subject to appropriate risk management.

To direct a strategy, ISO/IEC 38505 continues to advise governing bodies in directing the preparation of data use for future business development. The submission of proposals for innovative data uses is also encouraged - supporting a response to new challenges prompted by technologies in the Fourth Industrial Revolution that are outpacing regulatory frameworks.

Furthermore, the principle advises governing bodies to monitor the progress of approved data proposals to ensure that resources are allocated effectively, and the use of data achieves intended benefits. For the purposes of data storage accountability, this principle is a guiding start towards deploying assets to support a strategy. However, it is extremely important for organisations to strategically manage data by distinguishing data that supports the back-office business function of the organisation and free flowing data that guides decision making and direction setting. This is different from evaluating structured and unstructured data – this approach goes a step forward in further assessing the business objectives of different types of data and can also help mitigate its misuse. To that end, ISO/IEC 38505 can be used in conjunction with the function of data defence as part of an organisational strategy for data governance.

Data defence activities include downsizing risk, ensuring compliance with regulation such as rules governing the integrity of confidential business reports, and using analytics to detect and limit cybercrime. Strong regulation in industries such as financial services, aerospace or health care can move an organisation towards data defence – this would prompt the challenge for a CDO to establish an appropriate balance between abiding by strong regulation and using market data to respond to strong competition. This is rarely seen in practice as plenty of cases do not fall neatly into a single category of data use; for instance, a blockchain hedge fund manager is interested in using publicly and commercially available information captured in real time.

It all comes down to assessing an organisation's overall data strategy through accurate diagnosis, its regulatory environment, the data capabilities of its competitors, the advancement of its data management practices and the size of its data budget.

Principle 3: acquisition

Value for money of proposed investments is pertinent to help an organisation evaluate options for acquiring IT assets. This principle advises organisations to acquire IT assets with appropriate and suitable documentation, and adequate supply arrangements that support business needs. It also registers that organisations and suppliers share a reciprocal understanding of the organisation's intent in making any IT acquisition.

> Additionally, the 'monitor' pillar of the IT governance model in ISO/IEC 38500 (https://www.iso.org/standard/62816.html) advises governing bodies to monitor IT investments to ensure that they provide the required capabilities.

This principle is especially applicable to the acquisition and establishment of rapidly evolving data centres, supporting the continual growth of cloud services, with varying data management capabilities, across the world.

> In a 2012 study conducted by IBM, it was discovered that data centre operational efficiency had begun to move towards a consolidated approach through virtualisation to cut costs and dependency on physical servers.
>
> (Pane n.d.)
>
> With the emergence of cognitive computing technologies and cloud computing, major improvements to data governance and data science initiatives are set to go into effect as organisations realise the importance of controlling their data use while facilitating their ability to prepare for future data regulations.

International standards can guide companies in operating a strategic data centre consistently and in acquiring IT assets that can help them to optimise the server, network and storage facilities to maximise capacity and availability. Of course, the data centre example is not an exhaustive one: every form of IT acquisition must be assessed in terms of its return on investment; internal requirements such as the data culture pertaining to data storage cycles; and external pressures such as market forces, laws and regulations.

The international standards can also help governing bodies ensure that the relationship between stakeholders has room for flexibility to support changing business needs. They can further encourage organisations to acquire automation tools to improve service levels at data centres and to prepare roll-out plans that align with business goals. The standards will underscore the need for companies to build an enabling data architecture with structured formats that can be effectively managed, monitored and governed.

Principle 4: performance

Evaluation of the performance of IT-related plans is of utmost importance to a governing body in an organisation. Without the evaluation of proposed plans, the use and value of data within an organisation cannot be fully assessed. Similarly, risk assessment is also vital to continue the operation of the business arising from database activities. The international governance standards relating to IT and data clearly state that governing bodies should evaluate proposed plans and risks to the integrity of information and the protection of IT assets, including associated intellectual property and organisational memory.

These standards further advise governing bodies to assure that the use of data effectively supports business goals in line with the performance needs of an organisation, and that the performance can be evaluated, directed and monitored. This is to ensure that resources are sufficiently allocated as per agreed priorities and budgetary constraints, and that data is protected from loss and misuse. Such an approach is further advised to be galvanised through the monitoring of IT activities that support business, allocation of IT resources that are prioritised according to business objectives and the policies for data accuracy, and efficient use of IT to understand the value of the data and to improve the decision-making processes.

For governing bodies and organisations, it is important to view the governance framework and strategy around business performance through the lens of metrics.

In 2017, I attended a panel discussion organised by the Scotiabank Centre for Analytics in Canada, where it was widely agreed that metrics are one of the hardest aspects of data governance to grasp, but also one of the most important.

Metrics can reflect the alignment of performance with strategy in an organisation, so when managers are dealing with rogue data sets propagating in silos, metrics can articulate the relevance and value of data to help identify whether performance is meeting governance and business expectations. Working through the considerations of value, risk and constraint associated with the use of data at each point of the data accountability map described in the international standard for the governance of data, can assist with selecting suitable performance metrics. For example, metrics can track the number and nature of data proposals, the horizontal organisational risks according to each line of business (finance, marketing, human resources and so on) and each product/service offering, the number and use cases of IT assets and the effectiveness of every decision on business performance. Such key performance indicators (KPIs) can reflect the extent to which governing bodies are abiding by governance of data standards.

From a data storage standpoint, impact metrics can be established to track data defence activities, data centre operations, impact of poor performance in the past, change management plans through new on-premise and cloud storage strategies and the impact of improvement plans on the people within an organisation.

With the innovations occurring in the Fourth Industrial Revolution, the sheer volume of data stored and distributed across ever more complex network clusters needs to be organised, analysed and governed. With the guiding principles and data accountability map in ISO/IEC 38505-1, governing bodies and organisations can find themselves ahead of the curve with a governance framework supported by impact metrics to assess the performance of their data-related plans and decisions.

Principle 5: conformance

If the biggest changes and focus points of data storage of the past five years could be described in just a few words – themes from blockchain and micro services to private cloud, smart data, analytics and automation – they would be characterised as impactful, across the world. Addressing and understanding conformance in these emerging technology areas is a challenge.

ISO/IEC 38500 and ISO/IEC 38505-1 advise governing bodies to regularly evaluate the organisation's internal conformance to its framework for IT governance. The international standards also advise governing bodies to regularly evaluate the extent to which IT satisfies regulatory, legislation and contractual obligations, internal policies, standards and professional guidelines.

> During my analytics certification experience, I discovered data storage software that enabled me to actively manage information and recognise different types of stored data. I needed relevant data for proposal design to build a corporate innovation partnership, and it was simpler to do this with that software.
>
> This idea could potentially help organisations with distinguishing different types of data into use categories for governance and business development purposes, as explained earlier under the principle of strategy. Furthermore, such an approach can not only help the company itself, but also other organisations.

Conformance (compliance and regulatory conformance) is to be supported by appropriate reporting and audit practices which ensure timely reviews are carried out in a comprehensive and suitable manner. The disposal of IT assets including data must also be monitored to ensure that environmental, privacy, strategic knowledge management, preservation of organisational memory and other relevant obligations are met.

> Printing companies, for instance, have continued to incorporate sustainability into the fabric of their hardware equipment as well as managed print services. On one occasion, I showed a client how to capture documents to business workflows through one-button scanning while discussing a hardware re-manufacturing initiative that has saved over 52,000 tonnes of greenhouse gases and promoted social sustainability.
>
> In short, those printing companies have responsibly dealt with equipment disposal and also helped companies and individuals control costs and manage their data through the visibility of the use of print services and toners on a daily basis. This has reflected an embedded element of conformance in such companies to virtually any data governance framework for evaluation, direction and monitoring of business practices.

Conformance is easier said than done, but it is becoming increasingly measurable and achievable through the relevant avenues of legislation in countries where a lot can be learnt from fellow organisations with the same requirements to comply, white papers describing compliance planning frameworks, and existing and impending legislation packaged with official advice.

Principle 6: human behaviour

The respect attributed towards human behaviour is almost visionary in ISO/IEC 38500 in that it advises governing bodies to appropriately consider human behaviour in line with data cultures in organisations.

It is important that organisational data culture encourages the appropriate protection, sharing and interpretation of data. It is also vital to understand the behaviour of stakeholders. Naturally, a company may want to boost the attraction of their services among thousands of people in the form of website traffic indicators. However, if they are unclear about their outputs and outcomes, they may ignore useful ways to use such a metric to encourage better human interaction internally towards their data, which could impact business profitability.

Over time, organisations need to realise that properly considered and regulated human behaviour within a data culture can help them be more creative with metrics, be more honest about their data and become more accountable, and, in fact, more bulletproof if they are questioned on their behavioural integrity towards data storage.

When applying the ISO/IEC 38505-1 governance of data standard, organisations could consider the introduction of the role of an information literacy enablement representative to train employees on data culture. There is a noticeable shift in companies towards creating a better culture for employees – while their personal wellbeing and enjoyment at the workplace is of utmost priority, their impact on data use is worth highlighting to make them realise how important this is to their industry. With an increased sense of accountability, they could positively reshape data management and set an example for many to follow.

SUMMARY

Data governance is a call not only to help increase technology literacy among governing bodies, in order to assist businesses to remain abreast of modern business models, but also to sustain modern data flows and continuously innovate. With the international standards publicly available, it is hoped that voices of consent and dissent in the field of data governance are not maligned in the digital narrative but, rather, brought together so that people from different backgrounds and experiences can implement ideas in terms of service, data cultures, data ethics and data governance policies.

Instead of reacting to new data governance methods and pointing the finger of responsibility at one entity, businesses and governing bodies must proactively work collectively to support the digital nature of our sharing economy. The international standards will best be used when businesses and governing bodies establish effective ways to address the six principles of good IT governance in line with the data accountability map to track data vigilance.

Specifically, there is an onus on the governing body to ensure that decisions relating to the storage of data to drive value and reduce risk (such as decisions around sovereignty and the use of offshore services) are communicated throughout the organisation to ensure conformance.

7 DECIDE

Geoff Clarke

Whether it's written in a book or stored in some vast data centre, data on its own is of no use. Like any asset, we need to do something with data to make it useful – and that 'do something' is to make a decision.

In fact, we can go a step further and say that the end value of data is the value of the decisions that are made using that data.

But before we can make a decision – at least one that is based on facts rather than intuition – we need to extract the data from our data stores so that we have the right information in the right format. In other words, we need to have the facts in front of us in a comprehensible format so that we can make a decision based on them. This extraction and analysis of data is called the *report* activity in ISO/IEC 38505 because a common format for representing data is a simple printed report. Of course, there is often a great deal of science and technology involved in creating this report – and we'll examine some of the governance challenges with these tools.

The report will show us the facts in a comprehensible way so that we can understand them in the context of our decision scope. From that, we make or review a decision. This also involves bringing in other information (such as our experience, the objectives we have in mind, the time frames and resources available to us) and applying that to the information that is presented to us by the report.

Because the *decide* activity also involves bringing in additional data, it is almost an extension of the *report* activity; however, the governance issues of decision making are enough to highlight them as a separate issue.

The purpose of this chapter is to examine the appropriate governance that needs to be in place when making decisions from data. Applying the considerations of value, risk and constraint will assist an organisation in developing governance measures to significantly enhance data-enabled decision making.

THE VALUE OF DATA

We usually think of data as an intangible asset. If you purchase a customer list or a design specification, you could probably report that asset as having the value that you paid for it. But data that you've generated yourself, or insights that have been derived, will most likely not be seen on the balance sheet because they are too difficult to value.

Taking such a 'pure accounting' perspective on the value of data can be very misleading. For example, if you knew which horse would win Race 6 next Saturday, that could be very valuable information – but only if you placed a bet on that horse before the race was run. After the race, or if you did nothing with that information, its value to you, the prospective punter, would be zero. So, making a decision (to place a bet), taking action on that decision (placing the bet) and doing it within the specified time (before the race) are all necessary to gain value from that data.

Thus, data per se may have potential value, but a decision (and action) is required to realise that value.

This is no different from many other assets, where the value of the asset is simply defined as how much can you get for it when you sell it. And like other assets, you can sell its potential. As with the value chain of oil, data can be sold on, further refined or enriched. The end value for oil is the power that is derived from its use (whether that be its burning for power or its inclusion in other products such as plastics) but the end value for data is the decisions made from it.

The difference with data is that you can sell it, but still have it – in other words, the concept of data ownership is not particularly relevant in its valuation. What is more relevant is the 'use rights' of the data – and this is what is really bought or sold. Such rights may include copyright, reselling and distribution rights or privacy rights, which could reduce the potential value of the data by limiting the decisions that can be made from it. Additionally, it is likely that the rights you have on the data may imply an obligation on those that use it. In some cases, the obligations associated with the data might have us think of that data as a liability rather than an asset. For example, if the organisation processes personal health data, which generally has many imposed obligations in its handling, it needs to be very careful that the value derived from this data outweighs the obligations and risks that come with it.

AUTOMATED DECISION MAKING

Advances in computer science now enable automated decision making based on predictive models. These models are built using machine-learning algorithms and techniques from historic data and records of past success and failure.

These techniques shortcut the time and effort between data and decisions. They hold the promise of learning new patterns from the data, and learning new ways of predicting behaviour. Using tools and techniques, it is possible to automate almost every decision that is made.

Automated decision making happens everywhere – from the air conditioner deciding when to turn on the compressor, to very complex share-trading algorithms that buy and sell shares based on many different factors. Anyone who has driven a modern car knows that life-critical decisions are made by the car's brake system and airbags. For these everyday decision-making devices we are generally comfortable with the decisions that are made. There are several reasons for this comfort, including:

- The scope of the decisions made match the responsibility we have 'assigned'. For example, we don't expect the air conditioner to pay our bills. We don't expect the braking system to have the ability to switch off (rather than idle) the engine.

- For the most part, we can test different scenarios and reflect on the decisions made. For example, with the air conditioner it's easy to change the desired temperature. We also have some experience of how the device will react when it is unusually hot or cold. Similarly with the braking system – we can apply the brakes under different scenarios such as rain, snow, high speed, low speed, cornering and so on and measure the resulting decisions.

- Where we can't easily exercise decision making (for example, causing the air bags to be deployed) we rely on others to assert the decision-making capabilities based on laboratory testing.

- If there is ever a situation when an incorrect decision has been made, we rely on a post-analysis to be done by experts to understand why the decision was made. Not all devices have such 'flight recorders', but where critical decisions are made, we expect some form of audit trail.

Because of the increase in computational power, the reduction in cost through cloud computing, the ease of gathering new data and the tools that can analyse such data, the scope of automated decision making is expanding; and, as with many decisions, stakeholders are requesting more transparency in understanding how decisions are made – or at least how to correct a 'bad decision' and improve the decision-making process.

In fact, to maximise the effectiveness of machine learning or automated decision making, it is necessary to first understand the success (and failure) outcomes and the decisions that led to those outcomes. In that way, the decision-making process can be scoped, the decisions tested (either based on historic data or simulated data) and the outcomes examined to see if they offer the best solution to the defined problem. Machine learning algorithms then help to get closer to those 'best solutions' by analysing much more data than a human could.

As with the examples above, there are already existing governance mechanisms for 'feeling comfortable' about decision-making processes and for reviewing decisions when the result is unexpected.

THE GOVERNANCE OF DECISION MAKING

Using the maxim that the end value of data is to help you make decisions, we then need to understand what makes a decision a 'good' decision. This is because, like any plan of action, we need to clearly define what success looks like – or at least describe our end goal in the process.

Governance of decision making is, of course, part of the overall governance of an organisation. We start with a clarity of purpose for the organisation, understanding the needs of stakeholders (including owners, regulators, suppliers, customers and the environment) and then determining the strategy of how long-term value can be added to the organisation – within the available resources and risk appetite.

As shown in Figure 7.1, authority is delegated throughout the organisation to 'spread the load' of the decisions and actions that can be taken. Along with this thread of authority goes a responsibility for subordinate actions. The corollary of that responsibility is the accountability back up the chain to the board or governing body, noting that the board or governing body remains accountable to the stakeholders for the decisions and actions of the organisation.

Figure 7.1 Decision making in an organisation

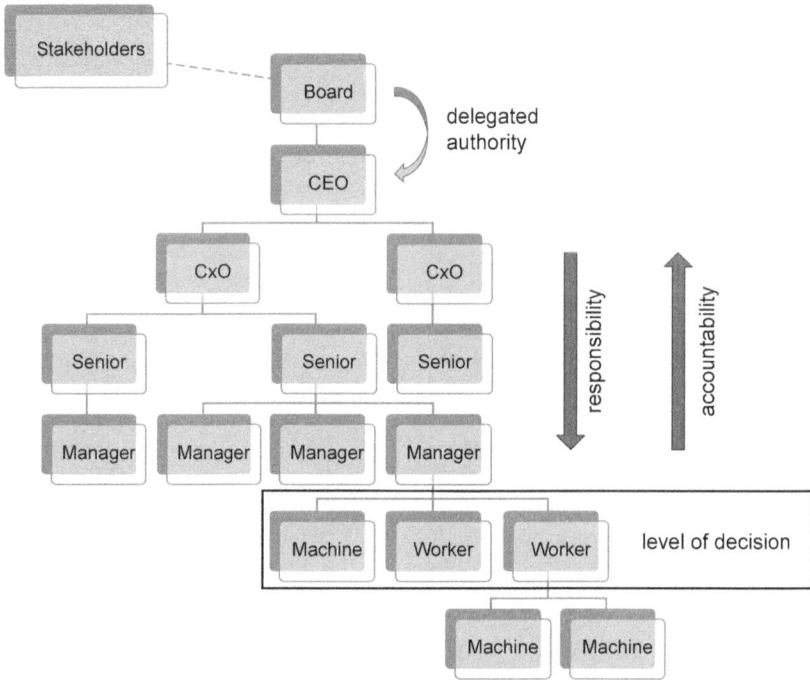

There are a number of other important factors to consider here.

Alignment to strategy

Decisions should align to the strategy for the organisation so that every action is a step towards the purpose of the organisation, while also keeping within the allocated resources, defined risk and other controls imposed by the organisation. Of course, not all decisions will be directly tied to the strategy, but keeping that perspective as part of the culture of the organisation helps with the efficiency and effectiveness of the organisation and helps to prioritise decision making appropriately.

Level of responsibility

Ensuring that the level of decision making matches the authority granted and responsibility associated with the decision is a critical element of good governance. Getting this match correct can sometimes be difficult. We often see simple examples of this in procurement, where different roles in the organisation have different purchasing power.

For example, a worker with a lower level of responsibility might be able to place a purchase order for items up to £1,000, whereas the worker's manager may have a limit of £5,000 and so on up the hierarchy. One of the issues with this particular example is that there is sometimes a mismatch between operating expertise and purchase power, which can lead to inefficient decision chains and lost agility.

Defining the scope and impact of possible decisions and matching those to the levels of responsibility of the decision maker is very useful in order to empower employees to act quickly and thus make the whole organisation more agile; but it can be difficult to specify such scope. To be able to take advantage of more automated decision making, this definition will need to become more clearly defined.

The decision-making process

The process of making the decision may be more important than the decision itself. For example, we know that every decision brings a risk and we also know that stakeholders are increasingly interested in transparency of process – and, in some cases, the decision made will be incorrect. However, if it can be shown that the process of arriving at the decision is 'good', then that may be more important than the resulting actions from the decision itself. In other words, the organisation needs to be agile enough to make decisions quickly, understand that mistakes will sometimes be made, learn from those mistakes, mitigate any damage and improve the process; but having a suitable and transparent process is the necessary starting point.

An example of this 'process must be good' scenario is in the setting of strategy for the organisation. If the organisation is a company in a very competitive market, then choosing a successful and differentiating strategy will be difficult because the efficiency of the market ensures that any obviously good strategy is quickly adopted or adapted by competitors. In these circumstances, stakeholders should not expect a fixed strategy that describes the innovations, good marketing, great business model and very good execution that gives the company a competitive advantage, but they will expect to see a good process of strategic planning with the acceptance of management reports, third-party input, focused questioning and an ongoing iteration of strategic thinking. If the board can show such robust processes, then this points to long-term success – and some 'bad decisions' along the way will be absorbed by the ongoing attention to the process.

Another example of the decision-making process can be found in car insurance. In assessing car insurance, you could list decision criteria and give a weighting to each to give you the cost for the cover; see Figure 7.1. Obviously, it's not quite as simple as this, and insurance actuaries have an art and science to work out the likely effect of such weightings.

The essence of machine learning is tools that can learn these weights from the data directly. This is done by iterating through the data and historic results to then find the weighting that best fits the model for predicting future behaviour or outcome. Machine learning can further assist the decision-making process by assessing much higher volumes and types of data, as well as determining a much larger pool of possible criteria.

Table 7.1 A simplified insurance rating system

Criteria	Weighting
Car is garaged at night	10
Suburb of garage	80
Drivers are aged over 25	100
Previous claims	50
Licence deductions	40

Table 7.2 looks at each of these criteria and debates their acceptability, highlighting what might be interpreted as 'unfair bias'.

Table 7.2 Possible biases in the simplified insurance rating system

Criteria	Possible bias
Car is garaged at night	Discriminates against people who can't afford garages
Suburb of garage	Clear socioeconomic bias!
Drivers are aged over 25	Blatant ageist behaviour
Previous claims	I have a right to be forgotten
Licence deductions	I've already served my time

The governance questions that arise here relate to the transparency of the decision-making process. In many cases, an insurance company is unlikely to go into much detail about the criteria, the weightings and the resulting cost for its customers. However, there does seem to be a trend towards transparency of decision making and this trend is driven by many factors, including:

- ensuring employee satisfaction;
- reducing the suspicion of bad management or governance practices (Glass 2016);
- exposing scientific methods behind decisions to increase participation and scrutiny.

So, it is likely that stakeholders will want to know more about the decision-making process – at least for decisions that directly affect them. The challenge will be to show enough to satisfy their needs while not divulging trade secrets, personal information or other sensitive data.

In simple decision processes like the car insurance example above, removing a possible bias such as the age of the driver will obviously have a big impact on the decision made because the weighting is so high. However, the solution success – providing adequate insurance cover at an economically acceptable price – may be very skewed; and, of course, removing all possible bias elements as inputs would result in a meaningless model since nearly all inputs could be perceived as a potential bias against a group of individuals.

In practice, the decisions on what constitutes unfair bias is determined for each market and applied near the end of the decision-making process to effectively remove or account for such bias. Unfair bias recognised at the outset can be excluded, but with learning systems unfair bias can be picked up along the way.

We can use the same technique for very complex processes (including automated decision making). Thus, while all data input can influence the outcome, we can decide which elements may constitute unfair bias (and possibly an unwelcome reinforcing behaviour) and account for such bias near the end of the decision-making process.

Regardless of the models used, and whether automated or not, accountability for decision making is a governance issue, not a technology one.

THE DATA VALUE CHAIN

We now understand that in today's connected world, data is much more valuable than it has been before, whereas in the past, an organisation operated its own data in a kind of silo, by creating its own data from customer records, manufacturing processes and the usual accounting requirements. The only 'value chain' for data was quite minimal because the only data that was moved between organisations was the 'system of record' information for orders, payments and so on.

Today, the data chain can be very complex as organisations and individuals trade or share data. As an example, Figure 7.2 shows four different organisations. The four organisations are represented by the four bubbles – one organisation that aggregates information, one that performs the analyse and refine function, one that performs the reporting function and one that carries out the decision function. If this were a financial services example, the 'aggregate' bubble could represent a stock market where information is collected from companies in the market, news reports could be bought from a provider and the market might subscribe to a credit agency rating report. It would then aggregate this information and share it with the public. Similarly, the 'analyse and refine' bubble might represent a financial analyst organisation that, through market interviews, report augmentation and other data gathering processes, analyses companies and refines the data it gathers. It then sells that information to others. In this case, the company represented by the 'report' bubble takes the publicly available information combined with the information it bought from the financial organisation and sells the resulting report to an individual. That individual then uses the information provided to decide what shares to buy or sell. This example is just a simplified version of what really happens, because some data will flow the other way and there will be very many sources for data.

Business processes within an organisation will likely use data that is at various points in the data value chain. As data becomes more valuable, understanding where in the data value chain the data you are using resides can help to prioritise the processes, make them more efficient and uncover savings for potential new revenue opportunities.

Figure 7.2 A data value chain

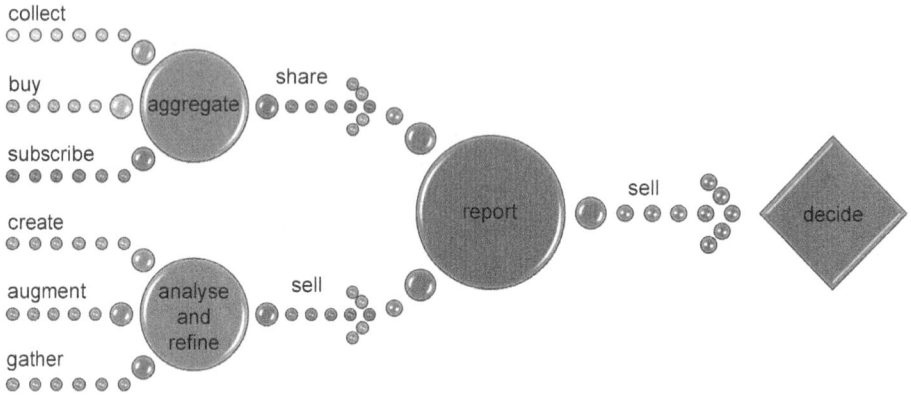

Let's look at some of the interactions in the process of making a pizza, for example, and the decisions that the parties make based on the data available to them. In Figure 7.3, which is a very simplified version of the many data flows in such a business process, the data value chain spans the suppliers of ingredients to the pizza kitchen, the production of the pizza itself, the delivery driver and finally the customer.

Figure 7.3 A data value chain for pizza production

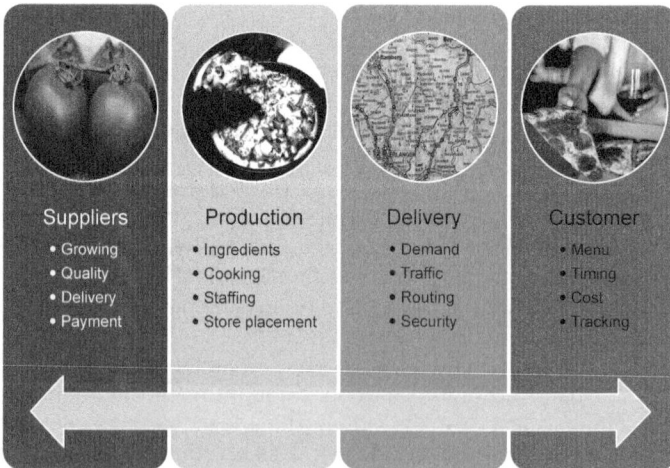

Suppliers	Production	Delivery	Customer
• Growing	• Ingredients	• Demand	• Menu
• Quality	• Cooking	• Traffic	• Timing
• Delivery	• Staffing	• Routing	• Cost
• Payment	• Store placement	• Security	• Tracking

Even in such a simple example, we can see the value of data at all stages and how that data is used to make many decisions. With modern data platforms, we can see how the customer could easily go online, compare menus and prices from various pizza places and then select or design the pizza of their choice. Many pizza kitchens will offer better, richer and more current data to increase their value proposition to their customers. Such data could include:

- reminders of previous orders from the customer;
- suggestions for new options based on previous ratings;
- discounts for ordering early;
- tracking of the actual pizza as it is ordered, cooked and in transit.

By collecting information from their customers, the pizza kitchen can then better predict demand (even down to the individual customer) and pass that valuable data back to their suppliers – who can then make more accurate decisions about production, delivery requirements and so on.

It could even be possible to bake pizzas in advance based on a prediction of demand, dramatically cutting delivery time. An alert to a regular customer stating 'we have just baked your favourite pizza and can deliver it in 10 minutes' may result in some overproduction, but might also increase overall customer satisfaction – and profits.

With an understanding of this simple data chain, we can see how the value proposition includes not just a tasty pizza, but the data associated with the pizza, its ordering and delivery. But that data value chain can be used another way as well. A 'pizza broker app' could allow a customer to specify their requirements, including type of pizza, price range and delivery time. Various pizza kitchens could then subscribe to such data feeds and submit offers to the customer, who would then decide on which to accept. Again, understanding the data value chain helps us to understand the business processes and their potential.

The data value chain also highlights some other issues.

Governance

There are governance implications at all points in the data value chain. The ability to use (and reuse) the data is central to this theme. As the value of these chains become more apparent, so too does the need to respect the privacy of individuals. Regulations such as Europe's GDPR helps to safeguard customers' personal details. Beyond the 'control and compliance' governance issues are the 'strategy and policies' issues that organisations need to plan for. We all know that the taste and quality of a pizza are just two of the data we use as buying decisions – so getting the whole picture of the data involved is important for the business and its strategy.

Data

The data exchanged (whether freely shared or sold) is not only used for simple decision making. In our example, data can include recipes (used to decide what ingredients to mix and how) and transport routes (which may vary based on additional data such as traffic conditions, time and weather). Such data may be consumed by people, but also by machines. For example, it's easy to see that the pizza broker app could be largely automated, or that the pizza production could be automated based on recipes. In other words, it's not only people that make decisions from data. Another example of this is 3D printing – where it is much easier to transmit the specification for a part and print it than ship the actual part. In this case, the 3D printer uses the 'recipe' to decide how to print the part.

Data SLAs

Data is critical to this value chain and we can expect to see service level agreements (SLAs) that support such situations. An example of this is to be found in the ISO/IEC 19086 standard on SLA for cloud computing (https://www.iso.org/standard/67545.html).

SUMMARY

Recent technology innovations have made it much easier and cheaper for all businesses and individuals to create, absorb and analyse data, but the real end value of data is the decisions that are made from that data – whether those decisions are made by people or machines. We need good governance around the decision-making process so that we can ensure that the opportunities and responsibilities associated with the power of data are properly applied.

From a business perspective, we need to ensure that data is consumed and distributed in line with our policies and commitments. Decisions should be aligned to our overall strategy, and the authority of the decision maker should match the level of responsibility associated with those decisions. We also need a review mechanism for decisions, to deal with unwanted bias – this will also improve our decision-making process.

Done correctly, these governance issues can and should be applied for automated decision making too, so that we can leverage such techniques to increase the volume, impartiality and analysis of data we use for decisions. And we will need good governance in place where the decisions made are used by machines (for example, air conditioners, printers, robots) as well as people.

Understanding what makes decisions 'good decisions' will become increasingly important for everyone in the data value chain. The increase in the use and value of data shines a new spotlight on the governance of the decision-making process, but the basic principles of good governance remain relevant and appropriate in this new data-centric world.

Before automated decision making, and decision making directly informing machines or devices without human interaction, it was key to understand, assign and review human accountability for decision making within an organisation. Now, with growing automated decision-making processes, data governance-driven decisions are vital because 'bad decisions' can move more quickly and have significant impact.

8　REPORT

Rohan Light and Frédéric Gelissen

This chapter is presented in two halves covering the theory and practice for developing governing body requirements to manage delivery, and the practicalities of introducing governance of data across the reporting function. Driving efficiency and accuracy in reporting should result in better quality and more timely decisions. Applying a governance framework over reporting data will ensure that reports inform decisions that set organisational direction and align with organisational goals, visions and mission.

REPORT: THEORY

Data is like light: we can think of it as both a wave and a particle – data is both 'something' and 'about something'. Boards must establish principles for the reporting of data that inform both qualities. A common business tactic is to get as much data (the something) as possible for 'insight' (the about something), but without putting thought into communication, organisation and decision making, all we end up with is an inert data lake. Lots of the something, but not much of the about something.

Effective reporting on data requires people to start, continue or stop doing something. It requires them to believe something to be true and change their behaviour. An effective report on data is not as simple as a 'financial statement for data'; it's more like a 'mass spectrometer for data'. This is because the data moving through and within an organisation is not homogenous. Two different datum combined create a third, different datum whose meaning can change our value estimate of the first two.

Data tends to crowd people out of the conversation – the discussion becomes about numbers – but organisations are full of people, and people speak in terms of values and beliefs. This means reporting on data is an exercise in preparing for communications between people on topics that move people. Data is specific where communication is a configuration. These configurations consist of a set of data that some people think is important and others think is trivial. People end up arguing about the abstract and lose sight of who they are. If the reporting on data just becomes about numbers, the opportunities for genuine transformation become limited.

This is a particular issue for the effective governance of data. Data is dehumanised and impersonal. The reporting on data needs to carry both economic and ethical signals simultaneously. All parts of the organisation that deal with data, which is every part of the organisation, will need to be able make sure their data use is both productive and responsible. This is no easy feat.

Reporting on data is subject to the instrument effect and confirmation bias. The former is where changes of measurement change what we can say about the meaning of the data. The latter leads us to interpret data to conform with what we expect. Controlling for these and other biases is an important task for organisations.

How we report on the value, risk and constraints on data will change depending on who is doing the measuring. Reporting on data value by finance, operational and change professionals will all be different. Deciding which professional group will set the primary lens for the reporting on data is one of the more critical governance decisions.

Terminology becomes critical for boards to navigate. Every profession deals with data and has their own specific language. 'A report' is different from 'to report'. Reporting 'on' data is different from the reporting 'of' data. Who you report 'to' is different from what you 'report'. A report can come with facts or no facts, truth or truthiness. A report can seem to be rich in information, but found to be poor in meaning. A report can fill 10 pages or consist of 120 characters. The reporting of data is fraught with challenges, so setting governance principles for the reporting of data is a critical leadership activity.

Effective reporting on data demands people's attention. Setting the rules around what we give attention to shouldn't be an afterthought. It shouldn't have to compete with everything else people think is important. It should be front and centre. This is because data has become the lifeblood of an organisation. In the same way people want to know that their pulse is healthy, so boards want to know about their data flow.

Boards must set the standards for reporting

Data is an organisational asset. Because boards have a duty of care to organisational assets, it is the board that must set the rules for the reporting on data value, risk and constraint. This observes the principle that it is the recipient of information who communicates. If the reporting on data value is broadcast by data scientists to a board that doesn't speak data scientist, then all the board will hear is noise. It is the board that must decide what the signal is.

A critical task for boards is to think through how to ensure that the economic use of data is also an ethical use of data. People process economic and ethical information in different parts of the brain. Organisations that use functional business models do the same. One business unit focuses on financial data while another focuses on 'conscience' data.

The challenge for boards is recognising that the data-enabled and digitally transformed organisation is a complex adaptive system. Traditional analogies are less useful than they used to be. Organisations are no longer armies, were never machines and few are the families their cultures claim to be. For boards, this means it will no longer be enough to have one part of the organisation in charge of conscience activities.

Large sections of an organisation can act in the economic interests of the organisation, but completely miss the point when it comes to the ethics of what they do. These failures can be failures in the governance of data because unethical practices can emerge from the way data has been manipulated.

The governance purpose for the reporting of data is to set the quality standards for creating, combining, interpreting and aggregating data. This is important because the data world tends to emphasise the quantitative. It is easy to lose sight of people and what is important to people. The value of data is dependent on the values of the organisation and the world it inhabits. What is quality to one organisation is rubbish to another.

Values and beliefs quickly come into play when the conversation turns to defining quality reporting on data. Without quality standards, reporting on data will become reduced to what can be counted. 'How valuable' degenerates into 'how many', and boards can lose perspective and context for their decision making.

Reporting is about communication

Reporting on data within organisations is about how different systems communicate with each other.

Reporting can degenerate into pushing around packets of information that only some people understand. The issue is that most people won't agree on what the most important elements of data are. They won't agree on what is mission critical because they have different perspectives on this, and will report on what they see as important, which often comes down to who they are and what they do. That's unsustainable for organisations seeking economies of scale or scope in the knowledge era. Effective governance on the reporting of data aims to fix this.

At its most simple, a report is a meaningful configuration of data. Note that meaning is independent of the message. For example, we know that our DNA carries our genetic code. We also know that we don't understand most of that genetic code, so the genetic data exists separately from our ability to understand it. In the context of the reporting of data, pushing out data reports that we think are meaningful is pointless if the recipient doesn't know the code.

A report is a configuration because it makes deliberate choices about what is in and what is out. This means reports hard-code framing effects for their organisations. Whoever sets the frame of the question prefigures the answer to that question. Because reporting on data must communicate value, risk and constraint, the right frame becomes crucial.

A report is a statement of what is important. What the board member thinks is important is likely to be quite different from what the customer-facing employee thinks is important. Both perspectives are equally valid. The reporting on data has to find a way to account for both. How an organisation configures a report sets an upper bound for its effectiveness.

Having all the data in the world won't be of any use if we can't communicate what the data means. We have to move data around and transform it to make meaning from it. Having lots of data can simply result in an increase in noise and meaninglessness. Boards are better off taking the time to set principles of communication. Throwing money at promising ventures that will 'realise the untapped value of data' is a poor strategy.

To realise the value of data, the board must have confidence in the means of communication within the organisation. Because communication precedes information, and information is independent of data, communication becomes the mode of organisation. In the same way we can use a bicycle, car or helicopter as our mode of travel, how we communicate the value, risk and constraints of data will determine the success of our organisation.

The meaning of what organisations report on data value, risk and constraint will always be encoded. The board must know the code. Because it is the responsibility of the board to set the rules on the governance of data, the board must also be the authors of the code. This is so they will be able to understand what the reporting means when it 'bounces back' after travelling through the organisation.

Communication is the mode of organisation

How an organisation reports on data tells the story of how the organisation communicates with itself. Every organisation is a grab bag of different systems, each system optimising to solve a different problem. Like the brain, each of these systems evolved at a different time and with different people and different intent. Like the brain, an organisation is a distributed processing system. Data moves around the organisation and no part of the system can understand what it all means.

Communication is the mode of organisation. Smart organisations are becoming more human, leaving impersonal communication platforms (e.g. email) for group chat platforms (e.g. Facebook for Business). Reporting on data will skew towards the impersonal, which means boards need to take care with how they establish the principles motivating the reporting on data. Boards need to know how the organisation is making room for the human in among all the data.

All organisations are wired differently. Data flows in different directions when comparing one close competitor with another. Organisations can feel very different based simply on how they evolved over time. This creates strong currents within an organisation, and data will follow those currents. Reporting on data should give boards an indication of what those big currents look like. To overlay a rational or diagrammatic data reporting protocol on an organic system will create a conflict, and the cultural system in place will win out over the elegant data reporting regime.

One of the important tasks for boards is balancing the data ecosystem within the organisation. This involves deciding what data flows to highlight. Some parts of the organisation will be bright with data, while others will be quite dark. Some data will flow like rapids, while others will be sluggish. It's a natural tendency to emphasise what is bright and fast, but boards should dig down deeper. Strengthening one part of the data ecosystem based on its reporting can make the organisation weaker.

Because an organisation is a distributed processing system, not all data reporting will be meaningful to each subsystem. Reporting on data has to make sure that the right data flows go to the right business units. The idea of producing multi-use data reports seems at first glance to be a good one. However, this approach to the reporting of data leads to a situation akin to what happens when the brain has to deal with multitasking: it results in information getting sent to the wrong part of the brain. The analogue for organisations is that multi-use reports increase the noise and drown out the signal.

For boards this means that reporting on data relies on understanding what different business units want to know. This goes to learning, and the reporting on data should identify what the learning appetite for each business unit is. Some business units will take the approach of getting as much data as they can. This will further increase the noise of their system and make effective communication even harder. The business unit might then request additional data analytics resources, but this will only be as successful as the weakest connection to complementary business units.

When business units are managed separately, the overall system can obtain a low effectiveness equilibrium. Those business units that are data savvy will request more resources. However, unless the adjacent business units receive complementary levels of investment, the gains at the enterprise level will be marginal. Making high levels of investment in an analytics unit won't generate high returns until associated service delivery business units are connected up. Reporting on data should show this mismatch of bright and dark parts of the organisation.

This drives managers to get as much data as possible without thinking through what it means. This complicates efforts to realise data asset value by obscuring the reporting on data value. Loss aversion is built deep into our psychology: we will do a lot to avoid possible losses.

Reporting on data needs to help different parts of the organisation prioritise conflicting demands. This goes beyond the pre-Big Data organisational mechanisms such as hierarchical organisation charts. As data-enabled technologies spread through the enterprise, network effects start to emerge as people connect past formal reporting lines.

Some organisations use matrix-style management structures, which are essentially stacked hierarchies. All of this increases the difficulty for business units to work out what is mission critical and what is not. Boards will need to think through how they will direct their senior management teams to configure reporting on data such that these conflicts are more readily solvable.

Organisations use data to make decisions

People quickly get swamped with data. Like multitasking, we tend to make a lot of our ability to make complex decisions; however, like the human brain, the decision-making capacity of an organisation has its limits. While some decision making can be automated, there will always come a time when people need to relate a range of disparate data together and make a decision. That decision will be highly uncertain and prone to becoming obsolete by fast paced change.

A common misconception with data is that the more we have of it, the better off we are. This isn't actually the case, and, while machine learning needs a lot of data to learn, quantity needs to be balanced with quality. Reporting on data needs to find a way to identify quality elements. With data analytics, garbage in becomes garbage out at scale – and people still have to make decisions based on that data. The qualitative aspect of data reporting becomes an important element in the enterprise assurance function.

The usefulness of data for decision making follows an inverted U function. Not enough data is qualitatively much the same as too much. The point where 'enough' data becomes 'too much' is around 10 data parameters for most people. The Goldilocks point (not too much and not too little) for data reporting is around five. Overloading people with data causes confusion and wastes time. If I supply 10 data points to inform a decision and only five are needed, I am wasting the time and resources of my data providers and my data users.

This reflects the practical optimum for people making lots of quick decisions under conditions of uncertainty, putting into perspective the claims that Big Data analytics will revolutionise organisations. There might be a revolution, but not of the good kind. Data overload is the enemy of good data reporting. Boards play a critical role in preventing bad decisions by establishing buffer limits on the amount of data in reports.

Those five data points that find their way to people in the form of a report need to help people relate what they do back to the organisation's purpose. And where the organisation is dealing with data about people (which is every organisation), this reference to purpose is critical to avoid problems when data about people causes harm to those people.

The data reporting regime needs to present people with the critical pieces of data that relate to critical decisions. This goes to the decision-making importance of good measurement. For complex adaptive systems like organisations, measurement is about reducing uncertainty on important decisions. It's not about counting discrete things. Because of the increasing velocity and acceleration of data within and around organisations, it's important to think about the veracity of data. How confident we can be about the accuracy of a datum is an important element of reporting on data. We aren't used to thinking in these terms, but all decisions come down to probabilities – and our brains aren't wired to deal with probabilities.

Summary

Boards need to establish broad decision-making principles around data to prevent reports becoming overstuffed with data bumf. This helps no one, especially the people close to the decision who need quality data reporting to support their decision making. The core principle of reporting on data here is that data moves vertically down the organisation with increasing specificity. The reverse also holds true: boards deal with only the most general data. But the people close to the decision need to understand the general principles behind the data reporting so that they can make their contextual points count.

A core principle for boards to establish for the reporting on data is that reports should shorten decision length. Because we live in a rapidly changing world, the value of expertise is falling. No one can keep up with the explosion of data in their disciplines, and to maintain expertise we must increasingly specialise. What this means for boards is that they must establish expectations that the data reporting environment is stable and orderly around the core elements of mission, purpose and value.

REPORT: PRACTICE

Reporting, just as other operational activities, is often dealt with in a very unstructured way in many companies, whatever their size, sector or location. Reporting must receive the same attention as the most demanding business processes of the enterprise, as it directly serves the business objectives by giving clear and factual insight on how the services perform, if and how security is sufficient and, as this book is concerned with, how data contributes to the success of the company.

Consequently, reporting must be considered as a process, and data reporting a domain that should be covered by the process. The ownership of the governing body is one of the most important key success factors of the implementation of the processes. They will therefore have to make sure the elements of the process and all enterprise constraints, market trends, legal obligations and operational capabilities will be taken care of in the implementation of the process. To achieve this goal, the governing body will write and enforce a reporting policy that will set the directions and scope of the process. The policy will be one of the tangible elements of the enterprise strategy regarding data reporting.

Developing strategy for reporting on collected data

Here, I will pinpoint the strategic topics the governing body will need to sponsor and enforce so that it's fed with valuable data reports enabling it to take relevant decisions for the enterprise.

The key topics and building blocks to consider are:

- PDCA principle;
- the roles and responsibilities (who is required?);
- the data landscape (where is the data, how is it treated?);
- a clever choice of KPIs and reporting information (what are the useful KPIs and what is the useful information to report?);
- the analysis of reports;
- the formalisation and communication of the subsequent data strategy (after reports have been analysed);
- following up on strategy deployment;
- the strategy on reporting tools.

PDCA
Reporting is a process that is key in the Plan Do Check Act cycle (also known as the Deming Wheel). Reporting has real value when decisions and actions can be drawn from analysis of the report. This is what the PDCA cycle aims for.

Reporting is a part of the Check phase of the cycle, but let's take a quick look at the four phases from a data strategy point of view.

Plan   The 'Plan' phase is where it all starts. After a first assessment of the situation regarding enterprise data, the governing body sets a strategic plan for data governance and management. Once this strategy is validated by all the relevant stakeholders (in business and IT), it can move to the next phase.

Do   The 'Do' phase is where the strategic plan is executed. All the projects that have been identified as part of the strategy are run. Once some of the projects give their first tangible results, the first data is available to be collected in a report and interpreted.

KPIs and relevant information to report have been identified, discussed with and validated by the governing body.

Check   All layers of the enterprise produce the reports in the 'Check' phase. The strategy-oriented KPIs and information are collected in reports that are tailormade for the governing body. An appropriate level of detail and the format of data presentation is defined and proposed.

It is likely, of course, that the quality of the reports will get improved at each turn of the PDCA cycle, just as for any element of the governance system.

The reports are analysed by the governing body as well as by some selected strategy advisors (internal or subcontracted data strategy experts). The result of the analysis is an explicit action plan, with action owners and deadlines, gathering all the necessary tasks that would improve data governance and management in the enterprise.

Act   The 'Act' phase is simply the execution of the actions by various teams under the lead of the action owners.

Once actions are finalised, the next turn of the PDCA cycle can start.

Roles and responsibilities
Reporting is at least a process and could certainly be considered as a service too. We therefore need to define the actors of this process, the customers of the service and what roles they must play.

Identifying the right people to collect the reporting data, analyse and present it in a timely manner, validate the reports and explain them to the governing body is key for the service to work.

Any service relies on the IT Infrastructure Library (ITIL®) four Ps: People, Process, Partners and Products (tools).

'People' is, without a doubt, the most important dimension of any service. The reason is that people run the process, run the tools, maintain the whole reporting service and, if designated people are not convinced of what they should do within the process, they will voluntarily or unconsciously sabotage or slow down the service.

'Partners' will, in many cases, get involved in the reporting process as subcontractors, and will often be implicated in data handling and treatment.

'Products' will ease the reporting process and make the whole service more efficient and faster.

The customers   Of course, in the frame of data strategy, the customers are the members of the governing body.

It is likely that, in small or medium sized organisations, data stewards are part of the governing body, while in bigger companies the governing body would delegate its stewardship to key people in the organisation.

As with any commercial activity, the seller needs to know its customers well. The provider of the report really needs to know the members of the intended audience, their level of knowledge, their paradigms and their objectives, to understand and comply with their expectations.

The governing body will often comprise the usual customer experience structure, gathering the CEO plus representatives from business (directors), finance (chief financial officer; CFO), information and communication technology (ICT) (chief information officer; CIO), HR and maybe risk and security. Some guests may be invited to review the reports, such as representatives from logistics, the legal department or data stewards.

Satisfying this variety of views is a challenge.

The providers   Report managers are people with a management role in the tactical and operational layers of the enterprise. They may be team leaders, process owners or process managers. They are accountable for the reporting activity, and play the role of the interface between the governing body and the data reporting organisation (reporting analysts from the business intelligence (BI) centre and various expert teams). The challenge of the report manager's role is to understand, on one hand, the need for synopsis and high-level information for the governing body and, on the other hand, the technical constraints and low-level requirements of the reporting analysts. Report managers will need to build a constant communication and message translation flow between these bodies.

Reporting analysts will be responsible for the technical aspects of the reporting process. They will technically apply the requirements described and explained by the report manager. They will also configure the tools and be the instigators of the evolution of the tooling to keep in constant alignment with the management requirements, and therefore with the needs of the governing body.

Data landscape

Every company has its own personal data landscape. The landscape is the result of a complex formula whose terms and parameters are the culture, habits, attitude and behaviour of internal and external collaborators of the company. It is combined with legal requirements, market demands and the customers' needs to influence how data is collected, stored, treated, distributed and disposed of.

Establishing a strategy can only be performed when you know how this landscape really looks. Would Napoleon or General Patton have defined their attack and defence strategy without having very precise and exact information on how the battlefield looked? Would they have dressed up a plan without knowing what resources were available and what their strength and weaknesses were? The answer is of course 'no', and you should easily conclude the same when setting up a data strategy.

It is obvious that the very first report the governing body needs to have in their hands is the data landscape. For the data reporting to be relevant, the enterprise must know what data it manipulates or stores, where the data elements are located and through which channels they flow. Without this architectural data picture, we can easily imagine that no reliable reporting is even possible.

Establishing a view on the data is not as easy as taking a picture. In your enterprise, data inputs, storage locations and outputs are numerous. You may also have data stored somewhere in an official location and 10 copies elsewhere in less controlled places (e.g. laptops, cloud drives, smartphones, USB keys). You may also have uncontrolled data transfers to subcontractors or internal departments. The IT department needs to draw this complicated data topography and present the map in a simple and understandable way to the governing body.

The data landscape is mainly composed of three major interrelated elements:

1. the information classification;
2. the treatment flows of sensitive data, highlighting its passage through the organisation;
3. a risk analysis.

We will develop them and briefly show how they contribute to data strategy.

Information classification   Information can be defined as a group of related data that, once put together, can produce a specific meaning for its user. A user can make decisions on an information item, while it is often impossible to make decisions based on an isolated datum.

Information classification aims to associate useful metadata to all the information items that are handled by the company. You may need to know what information is sensitive, of a private nature or critical for the company in terms of availability. You may also require some data to be fully accurate and some not. You will then classify the information items on their levels of confidentiality, integrity, availability, privacy and business criticality, among other useful metadata that you will exploit to bring value and precision to your data reporting.

Data classification is a subdomain of the ISO 27001 standard. It is one of the most difficult domains to implement, as companies tend to store and handle data in a quick and often unstructured manner.

When it comes time to classify data, many questions pop up, including:

- Where do we start?
- Do we have to inventory everything?
- Do we really have secret, confidential and private data?
- What about our partners and subcontractors? Are we responsible for what they do with data?

A few basic principles will help you to initiate the classification and progressively paint the big picture:

- **Do workshops with stakeholders:** If one person starts to classify data in their little corner office, the result will probably be very poor in quality. Information classification is a very good occasion to start a collaboration between the business, legal, security, risk and IT departments.
- **Start small:** Start with one team or one service. Do not try to cover too much in one go.
- **Focus on what is critical:** Starting small also means focusing on what is critical to the company. Start with what you know, and you will probably discover interesting things during the classification exercise.
- **Use well known tools and methods:** Some data inventory tools and techniques exist, such as Microsoft data classification toolkit, Spirion™, data discovery, Netwrix Auditor™ and many others, which can you can use for this purpose. You may also choose to call an expert to help you drill down into your databases and file shares to dig up treasures.

Data treatment flows   Once the information starts to be classified, it is time to figure out what your enterprise and its partners do with it.

You can produce a data treatment register (or data processing register) that gathers the descriptions of how data is processed inside and outside the enterprise. The same principles as for data classification can be applied here (do workshops; start small; focus on critical data first; use known methods and tools).

Mapping data processing can be eased by applying methods and notations such as:

- Unified Modeling Language (UML™) – for modelling data flows in applications and systems.

- Business Process Model and Notation (BPMN™) – for modelling data processes.

- Ownership, Business process, Application, System, Hardware, Infrastructure (OBASHI®) APMG International – for materialising the layers through which the data circulates: from the organisation, through business processes to the lowest operational and technical layers of IT.

- And many other architecture frameworks like TOGAF® and Zachman® (Zachman International).

Data risk analysis   Establishing a view on risks relating to data is a requirement of many standards and regulations, such as the European GDPR. However, it is also a best practice all enterprises should apply.

Data is more precious than gold. It also has many legal constraints around it, with very high financial penalties in the case of non-compliance to the law.

Each data treatment that handles critical data should be analysed and managed through a risk management process. You should know what the business impact is of losing, disclosing, destroying or altering the data. You should know what to do if the data is not available anymore.

In data privacy jargon, the risk analysis is called a Data Protection Impact Assessment (DPIA) or a privacy impact assessment (PIA).

This can simply be done through usual risk analysis methodologies such as EBIOS (French methodology: 'Expression des besoins et identification des objectifs de sécurité' meaning 'expressions of the needs and identification of the security objectives') and MEthod for Harmonised Analysis of Risk (MEHARI), among others.

Choosing the right KPIs and information

We see the landscape! The middle management has summarised and communicated this 'picture of the battlefield' to the governing body, which can now see what is in its hands. It is now up to the governing body members to express what they want to be reported on now that they are not blind anymore.

Choosing KPIs is another difficulty. Again, many companies have the misguided feeling that producing a lot of reporting data with a huge number of KPIs is always better because 'the more you know the more you can control'. However, what is true about KPIs is just as is true for any other information asset of the company: it must bring value!

KPI stands for key performance indicator. I believe everyone knows this acronym nowadays, but to tell you the truth I personally prefer to turn it around and define it as 'an indicator of performance that is key', or IPK. This way of approaching the concept of 'indicator', brought to me by my colleague and source of inspiration, Daniel Breston, simply emphasises the idea that your indicator must reflect performance that is critical for your organisation. Let's avoid measuring performance that does not directly and importantly influence the health and profitability of the company.

A useful technique to figure out if an indicator is good is to start from the end of the improvement process and ask yourself: What very important action will I execute if I know this indicator? Any key indicator results in tangible actions that bring value to the enterprise. If you have difficulties imagining valuable actions from the KPI, drop the KPI.

Reporting information and KPIs on data should consider all relevant elements for the enterprise. These elements can be:

- regulations and directives that require specific actions based on defined data parameters (e.g. data volumes, number of data owners, data risk level, incidents on data). Some examples are:
  - GDPR;
  - Network and Information Systems (NIS) Directive;
  - Privacy Shield;
  - sectorial regulations (e.g. health care regulations);
  - country and state laws (some countries ratify stricter laws that complement or overrule some general regulations);
- shareholder reporting (some strategic information will be required by shareholders);
- internal reporting for governance purposes;
- external and internal reporting for management purposes;
- public data reporting strategy towards end customers and data owners.

Analysing the reports
Now that the governing body has got a report set of a high quality, it's time to analyse and distil the essence of the reports.

Each member of the governing body should look at the reports from their own angle, using their own point of view. They should gather key learning points and potential actions. They should obtain advice from the report managers when clarifications are needed. The results of each personal analysis should then be correlated with the results from the other members of the governing body in a common strategic reflection (i.e. in a strategy set-up meeting).

It would not be good practice to discuss the reports directly in a one-shot strategic workshop as some members may be significantly influenced by others and fail to give their own opinion and directions.

Formalising and communicating the strategy
The reporting strategy is not different from any other part of the enterprise strategy. It must be formalised so that it is understandable by the people who will have to translate it into tactical and operational plans. This formalisation can take as many faces as there are target groups receiving the information on strategy. The five main strategy forms can be as set out in Table 8.1.

Table 8.1 Communication strategy and target groups

Form of the strategy communication	Target
A high-level plan with few details and big time objectives.	The whole company. Distribution on the intranet, on posters, etc.
A high-level plan focused on the benefits for the company and shareholders.	The shareholders.
A detailed plan with clear objectives.	The middle management so that tactical and operational plans can be proposed.
Focused parts of the plan with selected details.	The partners and subcontractors.
High-level information. Selected commercial topics.	The customers. For informational and marketing purposes.

Communication is often not as easy as it seems. To ensure the reporting strategy will be understood and translated into sound actions giving the expected results, the objectives of the strategy should be cascaded from layer to layer in the organisation.

Strategy follow-up and continuous alignment

All involved actors will need to decide how they can contribute to the reporting strategy. The contribution must also be formalised by each of the involved individuals. All documents that will be produced should be approved, stored in a central location and a periodic follow-up on all the proposed objectives should be executed to evaluate the performance of each employee, each team and each department.

Subcontractors will usually be evaluated through the projects they participate in and the services they provide, but they may also be assimilated as employees (and therefore follow the same process as internal people) if they hold an outsourced enterprise process. For example, if a pharmaceutical company outsourced its drug production process, the objectives would apply to the outsourcing company too. The outsourcing company would have to define how they would contribute to the strategy.

It is very important that each stakeholder sets their own objectives, defining how they will contribute. If objectives are imposed on them, it is very likely that many of them will be overlooked or simply put aside.

The reporting tools strategy

In many big companies with many business and IT teams, the tooling architecture often tends to be messy, if there is something one can call an architecture at all.

Fast growing companies will certainly make tooling choices without a transversal view on the organisation, the processes, the services and their related needs. Each team will likely choose its own tooling based on its own few, very specific needs. This results in a redundant tooling architecture, high licencing costs, maintenance problems, communication difficulties between technical teams (as they do not have the same tool experience) and big issues when reports must be built, as all these applications do not 'talk' together.

Tooling is never the solution to the problems of a company. Tooling only exists to support existing processes and make them more efficient. This means that before implementing a tool, there must be a process that is able to run without sophisticated applications (this could be paper sheets or basic electronic tables or forms).

Reporting is a process, too, and the same question must be raised and answered: Do I need a tool for reporting? The answer may be that some very isolated information can be manually reported and some not.

Of course, the choice of having a nice tool for reporting will depend on the amount of data it needs to handle, the need for correlation and calculation as well as the design requirements of the report (e.g. graphics, automated online dashboard publishing).

The strategy on reporting tools will need to consider the following parameters:

- maturity of the processes (IT and business);
- data sources;
- data volumes;
- data types;
- data processing (how complicated the processing is, report design needs);
- report communication vectors (online dashboard, distribution automation);
- interface needs (with existing tools and applications);
- technical constraints (what applications and frameworks must be in the scope);
- organisational and competency constraints (who the actors are, what technical skills they need to have);
- budgets for tooling and business cases;
- data feed and data stores.

Developing a policy for reporting on collected data

Although policies are often simple and short strategic documents, their development can be time-consuming in big organisations, where many governance body members must give their feedback, validate their contents and commit to the subsequent deployment of the policies' rules in the enterprise.

Many organisations do not even really understand what a policy means and what the implications are of their implementation. We will therefore go through the essential elements of the development of a policy in this section.

What is a 'data reporting' policy?
A policy aims to formalise the essential rules for the enterprise. These rules will have to be applied to design and implement the related processes and all subsequent tactical and operational procedures. It is important, therefore, that the data reporting policy is written, or at least validated, by the governing body, as the policy represents a sort of blueprint for the building of the reporting process.

The reporting policy should be short and clear. It needs to be understood by the various target implementers.

The data reporting policy can also be integrated into a broader policy on reporting the scope of the entirety of enterprise activities (e.g. a service reporting policy).

Defining the objectives of a data reporting policy

The first section of the policy must set the objectives. The data reporting policy will describe, in a concise but thorough manner:

- What data reporting in the context of the enterprise is.
- What the challenges are.
- Why the enterprise must perform data reporting.
- What the benefits are.
- What the risks are if data reporting is not done.

Examples can be given if the text remains concise and clear. The 'objectives' section should not take more than half a page.

Context and challenges: describing the context, you can remind the audience of the data types the enterprise must handle, the volumes it needs to manipulate, the variety of data locations, the legal obligations that need to be adhered to and the main requirements of the enterprise's customers in terms of data treatment and data reporting.

You will also summarise the challenges the company will be able to address by applying the rules of the policy.

The benefits: you can describe how data reporting will contribute to the success of the company, how it will help in taking good decisions and lead it in the right direction. You can explain how data and data reporting can bring value and an increase in finances.

The risks: starting from a preliminary risk analysis, or simply from the benefits, you should very briefly describe the risks pertaining to data and data reporting. You should describe what could go wrong if there is no or erroneous data reporting. Financial, legal, operational, reputational, health and safety risks should be considered in the risk description.

Defining the scope of the policy

The perimeter of the data reporting policy must be set. You will need to define what is in scope and what can be left out of it.

You need to define if these elements are 'in scope' or 'out of scope':

- data (some data types may be critical or address significant risks, and some not);

- services and/or business processes (some business processes may or may not participate in the vital and strategic functions of the enterprise);
- sites (some geographical entities could be out of the area of responsibilities of the governing body or could already have their own policy);
- specific systems and databases (some systems and databases may contain and handle data that is not relevant for data reporting, e.g. development or test environments).

Defining to whom the policy applies
Your target audience must be chosen appropriately. You will choose what roles and functions in the enterprise must read and understand the policy as they will have to apply it and, more than likely, turn the policy rules into tactical and operational actions.

> Having the audience defined is an opportunity to set the vocabulary and writing style of your policy. You need to choose your words so that your audience understands the messages that are outlined by the policy.

Data reporting will usually have an audience chosen among:

- data analysts (internal and external BI/reporting experts);
- upper and middle management;
- process owners;
- data stewards;
- supplier service managers (relationship managers from suppliers);
- governing body members.

Addressing the right topics in the policy
The data reporting policy will set the overall rules for data reporting. Referring to the ISO/IEC 38505-1 standard will help you to figure out what topics to address.

You will need to define rules and directives for data reporting on:

- **Value of data:** The governing body should influence and enable management, as well as the whole organisation, to extract value from data using the most appropriate methods and technologies. Adequate resources should be made available to make this possible. Four dimensions must be considered:

  i)   **Quality:** The expected level of quality of the data as well as required quality indicators should be defined. The level of quality should be aligned with other dimensions of the reporting (e.g. data classification) to define what data type should be reported with high accuracy (i.e. precise and exact data) and what data does not require high reporting standards to make sound decisions (exact data with less precision).

ii) **Timeliness:** Making the decision at the right time is key for many organisations. The requirements for timeliness should be defined. Multiple data reporting issues may be required (monthly, weekly, daily or even in real time with automated action taking) and, again, the type of data will influence the directives for timeliness as some of them may require very frequent lookup and decision making and some not.

iii) **Context:** Some external or internal factors as well as some correlated data may influence the reporting requirements. As an example, if there is a publication in the press that confirms an increase of cyberattacks on your type of company, you will probably require the reporting on intrusion detection data to be monitored more closely than usual. If a competitor launches a new product on the market you will probably modify your data reporting to figure out rapidly what to do to counter a possible market share loss. The data reporting policy will define rules to enable the organisation to quickly respond to this kind of need.

iv) **Volume:** Having sufficient data volumes will bring confidence in the statistical results of data analysis. The policy should set directives on required minimum data volumes for the governing body to take relevant decisions. The way high data volumes must be analysed and relayed back to the governing body should also be defined. The report must remain clear and concise for quick decision making.

- **Data risks:** The governing body should clarify and emphasise the context of data, including how company culture influences the consideration and use of data, and consider potential misuse and misunderstanding around the aggregation and interpretation of data. Three topics must be covered:

    i) **Management:** Reporting on how data is managed (process KPIs) and how data is at risk are key elements for the governing body to make decisions on the way to handle the security of this data and to ask for security management changes in the enterprise information management system.

    ii) **Classification:** Classification is probably the most important element of the strategy. It is the cornerstone of data reporting and more generally of data governance and management. Defining rules on classification and reporting on it will condition all the other requirements and actions. Rules on data inventory, qualification, classification and accountability will serve as a base for all decisions. Data reporting on classification will enable the governing body to keep an eye on how the enterprise evolves in terms of treated data (what the new data are and what challenges and risks these bring, and what the obsolete ones are).

    iii) **Security:** Once data is inventoried and classified, it is now time for the governing body to give itself the means for sound decisions on the security of data. The enterprise has the mission of treating the data safely. This is even more important when data is sensitive. The Privacy Shield and, more recently, the European GDPR bring legal constraints on the security of data. The governing body therefore needs to watch over the data processing in compliance with these regulations. Defining rules for reporting on data security (incidents, unauthorised access, integrity loss, etc.) is mandatory. Standards such as the ISO/IEC 27000 series, NIST and regulations such as GDPR will help you to fulfil your reporting objectives.

General and sectorial regulations (such as the good practice quality guidelines in the pharmaceutical and medical sectors) or local country laws force medical and pharmaceutical enterprises to handle data with high quality and safety standards, as this information may have a social impact if revealed to the public and health impact if integrity is lost. For example, an error on a drug label can be lethal for a patient.

- **Constraints:** The governing body must make sure that the links between data and its constraints are established. This is critical when data is aggregated from different data sets. The constraints can sometimes bring a heavy load of work for the enterprise. It is the duty of the governing body to define the relative importance of each of these constraints. Three subjects must be considered:

  i) **Regulations and legislations:** We have already mentioned Privacy Shield and GDPR above, but many other legal constraints may exist in the context of the enterprise. Contract clauses with the customers, service contracts with partners and suppliers and internal employee contracts are also constraints the governing body will have to consider when setting the rules for data reporting. As an example, your company (the data processor) needs to formalise its engagement with data owners (your customers) to process their data within a certain scope and with clearly defined finalities. The data owners will need to consent to these engagements of processing before letting the enterprise collect and handle their data. The governing body will have to monitor that the enterprise still respects its engagement over time. If not, corrective and preventative actions will need to be decided and executed. One of the actions may simply be to change the engagement text and ask for the consent of the data owners again.

  ii) **Societal:** Societal engagement, the will to show professional respect to the enterprise's workforce and the choice of complying with ISO 26000 ('Social responsibility') will require appropriate reporting to the governing body too. Societal engagement can be part of contract clauses with customers or internal rules and may also constitute a commercial differentiator (especially for companies belonging to regions of the world where the respect for workers is often criticised). It is then of the utmost importance to prove good implementation and the continuous improvement of societal measures and to set up a data strategy aiming to demonstrate these facts.

  iii) **Organisational:** The organisation of the data processor is influenced by the complexity, the volumes, the quality and the security requirements linked to data. The governing body will need to set the human resource strategy in accordance with the data treatment constraints of the enterprise. Reporting on the necessary technological evolutions and the complexity of data flows will influence the hiring of BI experts, database administrators, data architects and other specific technical profiles. Data volumes, the number of databases and the reporting complexity will probably condition the number of needed experts to a certain extent. The profiles and number of quality and security experts will also be conditioned by the data situation. Sound reporting will then contribute to choosing the right strategy.

Implementing the policy for reporting on collected data

Implementing a policy requires rules to be explained, understood and then converted into sound actions. Implementing the policy for reporting on data will consist of designing and deploying the processes, procedures, tools and organisation. It should be managed with a project management mindset for better control.

An implementation project should consider the following:

- appointing the implementers;
- monitoring implementation progress;
- implementing the process for reporting;
- reporting tools for data;
- archiving and retention of reports.

Appointing the implementers of the policy

A data reporting policy is just a set of useless rules if not communicated appropriately to the right people. Once the policy is written, the owner of the policy and the governing body need to distribute it to its target audience, verify good understanding of it and enforce the formalisation of a plan to implement the rules in the tactical and operational layers.

Implementing the policy will require working with the process owners and the managers of the reporting teams (such as BI centres of excellence, for instance). The managers and owners will analyse the gaps between what is in place and what is required in the policy. They will then gather all their observations into a plan, where they will be transformed into actions with associated action owners and due dates. Some actions may be significant in terms of complexity and workload. These actions will likely be turned into projects.

The plan would ideally be approved by the governing body or by at least one of its members.

Monitoring implementation and following up exceptions to the policy rules

The execution of the plan needs to be periodically reported to the governing body for decision making on the issues and evolution of the plan. Governing the data reporting implementation plan, just as you would do for any other strategic project, is key for the success of the process operationalisation.

The implementation of a policy is always subject to discussion with the operational teams. Operational teams have constraints that are often not taken into consideration when writing the policy document. Each rule of the policy should be considered as an objective to attain, but, in the set-up, some financial, technical or organisational difficulties may be raised, forcing operations to report exceptions. It is good practice to maintain an exceptions log and put a simple exception procedure in place. The purpose of doing this is simply to record the situations where the enterprise cannot comply with a rule and to record what it will do to work on it until compliance is achieved. Derogations may also be approved by the governing body within the exception procedure when compliance cannot be reached with reasonable actions. The derogations should be reviewed periodically by the governing body and the operations team to allow for opportunities to solve them.

Implementing the process for reporting

As mentioned earlier, the first key action of the data reporting policy implementation is the data reporting process. The process will not be developed here, but it should apply the requirements of the ISO 38505 standard to reach a good level of organisational maturity in the handling, use and interpretation of data.

Incorporating the ISO 38505 requirements in the service reporting, or any other governance reporting, process will most probably make it fit for purpose. It may also bring in elements to improve the current process, as reporting on data is at the heart of overall service and process (KPIs) reporting reflections. Better governance of reporting data will lead to more efficient and more reliable decision making.

Reporting tools for data

Many tools have been developed to help data analysts to report on data. In this section we will provide some examples of the most popular tools.

Most applications come with their own reporting functions or modules, but they may be limited and not flexible at all. This is why data analysts and BI specialists prefer to use specialised tools for exploiting data directly from a database or to manipulate copies of these data injected into data warehouses or data lakes.

The tools can be classified into four categories based on the reporting context:

1. report creation;
2. analysis;
3. data mining and statistics;
4. unstructured data reporting.

Report creation   The creation of reports requires software that can design and generate good looking and easy to use report layouts. These generators transform data into human-readable reports.

Analysis   Analysis is the manipulation of data to create data sets and combinations of data that can be used to produce sound reports that are real decision-making enablers.

The best-known solution for data analysis and manipulation is probably SAS®. It is a language and a set of software packs that allow statisticians and reporting experts to transform raw data and select what is relevant from that for useful reporting.

Elastic Search™ is probably the most famous solution for all types of data management activities when data is unstructured (such as web pages, emails, videos and all types of data that do not fit into the usual 'row and column' structured database style). The solution can integrate, store, manipulate and analyse data.

Data mining and statistics   Data mining tools are very good at extracting the essence from large amounts of data (Big Data) to generate new, valuable information. Here, again, we will find SAS and Elastic Search, but they compete with the big players such as Microsoft and its SQL Server™, Oracle® Data Mining, Apache Spark™, IBM® Cognos and many others.

Unstructured data reporting   Reporting from unstructured data requires sophisticated tools that can extract important information from the messy mashup of data. They may use artificial intelligence and machine learning to enable the creation of useful reports or to make automated decisions based on the results of their analysis.

Again SAS, DataRobot® and Elastic Search are the best positioned tools to execute these tasks.

> Time moves fast, and technology evolves even faster. I therefore suggest that you frequently explore the market and search for new, interesting solutions that meet your data analysis and reporting needs.

Archiving and retention

Reports on data are also considered data themselves and must be managed as such. All the principles of this book will then equally apply to the data reports.

The reports should be:

- accessed securely (e.g. secured connection if accessed remotely);
- stored in an appropriate location with adequate rights (strict access control) and protections (e.g. encryption);
- backed up, with adequate security measures in place to protect the back up system (e.g. backups separated from production data, tape refreshes, encryption, external storage);
- archived if required (if report must be kept for a long time due to legal, contractual or sectorial obligations).

Types of reporting

For reporting to be effective, it is useful to identify your target audience groups and the reporting types appropriate to them. Table 8.2 gives examples of the abstraction levels that should be considered regarding types of report and the level of confidentiality of the information that would be reported.

The way these reports would be distributed should also be considered. Information classification will therefore be linked to data (or information) distribution measures, such as encryption and password protection, for reports of a higher confidentiality.

Table 8.2 Reporting types per confidentiality level with target audience

Report type / medium	Target	Confidentiality
Intranet dashboard or video Posters on walls Internal displays	The whole company (employees and people working inside the organisation)	Medium
Paper report Electronic private dashboard	The shareholders	High
Paper report Electronic private dashboard	Upper and middle management	High
Paper report Electronic private dashboard	The partners and subcontractors	Medium / High
High-level information Selected commercial topics	The customers For informational and marketing purposes	Very low

Methods for distributing confidential reports could be storing the report in a restricted access folder, publishing the report in an access-controlled application or portal, or distributing the reports in sealed envelopes, for example.

Report on security

As data is the fuel of the enterprise, it is of course crucial to know the status of security controls around it. You do not want your engine to stop working.

Reporting on security requires covering the three dimensions of information security (CIA):

- data confidentiality;
- data integrity;
- data availability.

Having sound reporting enables the governing body to sense if the security measures in place are efficient and effective, and also shows if the associated processes run smoothly in the case of an incident involving critical or private data.

The European GDPR requires that incidents involving private data be reported to the relevant authorities within 72 hours from the time the incident is discovered. The data user should also be made aware of any issue with their personal data if this will affect their private life.

The governing body will not need detailed information on security (such as technical details on distributed denial of service attacks or brute force attempts[1]); the number of incidents impacting crucial data and the strategy to fix the related issues will be more useful for them as they will have decisions to make on projects and budgets to continuously improve information security. The degree of obsolescence of security systems and the vulnerability of the enterprise information system will also be strategic indicators for investment validation.

> Major information security incidents should be immediately reported to the governing body for them to decide whether the crisis, disaster recovery plan (DRP), business continuity plan (BCP) and specific communication procedures must be invoked (refer to ISO 27035 for security incident management).

Summary

Reporting on data is an operational process that directly feeds the governance system of the enterprise. It requires a strategy and tactical elements to be put in place to bring added value to the company.

Reporting will enable the governing body, as well as managers, to make the cycle of continuous improvement turn (PDCA). It will also help them to identify risks and opportunities.

Reporting on data is the key process for designing the data landscape and allows the information to be classified, which will be the starting point for taking measures to protect and use data appropriately.

The main purpose of reporting on data is to produce governance reports that address the needs of the governing body and enable them to make sound decisions on all analysis results that relate to data.

The strategy on data reporting must be formalised and communicated efficiently to get the entire organisation, including internal and external actors, aligned on the objectives related to data. This strategy must be implemented through a well-prepared policy and tangible implementation actions managed with a project management mindset.

The deployment of this strategy must be monitored and adjusted continuously to take account of changes in the data landscape.

---

1 Distributed denial of service (DDOS) attacks consist of saturating a service with requests to block it (take it down). Brute force attacks aim to discover passwords using specific hacking tools.

9 DISTRIBUTE

David Sutton

As with all areas of the governance of data, distribution of data – or distribution of the information derived from it – must consider the three aspects of governance:

- the inherent value of the data: to whom it has value, and why;
- the risks associated with its distribution;
- the constraints that may restrict its distribution.

Although the chapter heading – and indeed the title of this section of the ISO/IEC 38505-1:2017 standard – is about distribution, it is worthwhile noting that the term is only relevant from the perspective of the distributing organisation. From the perspective of the consumer it is about the retrieval, reception or acquisition of the data, and from the distributing organisation's perspective it can also be about sharing data. Good governance must consider both points of view.

THE HIERARCHY OF DATA

In order to better understand the value of data, it is important first to discuss the nature of the beast. Data may simply be individual facts, such as time, temperature, cost or a telephone number, or it can be a collection of facts, such as name, address, email address, telephone number and details of orders placed, which when brought together provide the next level in the hierarchy – information. We may then take these pieces of information and aggregate them for a large number of individuals, which provides the next level – knowledge – and it is in their ability to use this knowledge that organisations are able to make decisions. As we rise through each level of the hierarchy, the value of the data increases, while its volumes generally decrease.

Therefore, while we refer to 'data' throughout the chapter, we may also infer that we are also considering the distribution, sharing, retrieval, reception or acquisition of both information and knowledge, depending on the hierarchy level.

BASICS OF INFORMATION SECURITY

Before we examine the mechanics of data distribution governance, it is worthwhile taking a very brief look again at the fundamental aspects of information security, which, since they underpin the risks discussed later in this chapter, will have an impact on the distributing organisation's decisions regarding what data may be distributed.

- The first aspect is that of **confidentiality**, which broadly reflects the need to ensure that only those who are authorised to acquire or receive information are able to do so.

- The second is that of **integrity**, in which the accuracy, validity or correctness of the data is considered. Data integrity implies that, once recorded, data is not altered in any way by unauthorised persons or systems; to do so would be to compromise the value or usefulness of the data. Although not specifically considered in the traditional information security definition, integrity must also consider whether the data has been acquired lawfully and possibly with the consent of an individual who is represented by it.

- The third and final aspect is that of **availability**. Data is worthless if it is not available to those who require it, where and how they wish to receive it and at the time they require it.

MODELS FOR DISTRIBUTING DATA

There are two basic models for the distribution of data. The first of these models is of free access, in which consumers may obtain selected items of the distributing organisation's data at no cost. This model also covers distribution to consumers of the data within the organisation itself and to consumers in partner (business-to-business) organisations, for example insurance companies regularly share information on customers with other insurance companies as a means of reducing fraudulent claims.

The second model is one in which consumers must at least register or subscribe in order to receive data, or in many cases must make some form of payment in order to receive it. An example of this type of model is that of genealogical research organisations, in which subscribers can search for details of family history. Those who simply register on the websites are able to view a limited amount of data, while those who pay an annual subscription will have access to significantly greater volumes of data as well as additional data sets.

The decision regarding which of the two models to adopt – or indeed whether to use the free model for some data and the registered/paid model for other data – rests with the governing body of the distributing organisation and will be based on a number of criteria, such as:

- Whether the data is suitable for public dissemination, or is of a confidential or sensitive nature. For example, data that provides weather forecast information would be suitable for general public dissemination, whereas data about an individual's financial affairs would not.

- Whether data is of considerable commercial value. In the example above, weather forecasts are generally provided at a fairly high level of granularity and show weather by the hour. For a more detailed forecast – say by five-minute intervals, and providing considerably greater detail over an extended period of time – it would be perfectly reasonable for the meteorological service to make a charge.

- Whether data is intellectual property with less commercial value, but is expensive to develop and may take many months if not years of work – as in the example of international standards, in which case payments will help to offset or even recover the costs of development.

- Whether the data represents a means of maintaining a database of existing or potential customers, as in the case of an organisation that regularly publishes articles on subjects that will be of wide interest, and whose readership may well purchase a product or service as a result.

Data distribution models are not always used in the same way around the world. For example, the BSI and the ISO require payment for copies of their standards, whereas the American NIST takes a different view and makes all its standards freely available.

It is, of course, important to note that national and international legislation may heavily influence the choice of model, especially where data protection legislation is in place, and where the data concerned is of a personal or sensitive nature.

Value

Before any distribution or sharing of data is undertaken, it is vital that the organisation develops and adopts a data distribution policy, which must align with the organisation's strategic intentions.

The value of data can increase greatly when it is converted into information or knowledge. In this section we will examine the kind of value that data exhibits and those organisations and individuals to whom it has value, remembering of course that if the confidentiality, integrity or availability are compromised, much, if not all, of the data's value will be lost.

However, the quality or usefulness of the data is also key, since consumers of the data will only be interested in acquiring or receiving it if it is fit for purpose. Another aspect of quality is that of the volume of data being distributed. Too much or too little data made available may detract from its value – a small volume of high-quality data will always outrank a larger volume of data with a lower quality!

Paying consumers, especially, also have a right to expect the data to which they subscribe to be available in a timely manner. It would be useless, for example, to be told that a severe weather incident was due to occur some time after it had actually happened – in some cases, delays such as this could even be a matter of life and death.

Clause 4.2 of the ISO/IEC 38505-1:2017 standard (responsibilities of the governing body) states:

The key focus of the governing body's role in the governance of data is to ensure that the organisation obtains value from investments in data and associated IT, while managing risk and taking constraints into account.

Possibly the most obvious example of value is that of financial value, where data can be sold for money or perhaps traded for other data. In situations where data has a financial value, it stands to reason that the organisation should take steps to protect it and prevent the financial or commercial loss that would otherwise ensue. For instance, the leaked copy of a new book would deprive not only the publisher of a significant amount of profit but also the author of their royalties.

Academic value is often a precursor to financial value, in that academic research will often result in the development of something that can be sold, for example research in the pharmaceutical or petrochemical industries frequently takes a long time, but once a new drug is developed or a new oilfield is discovered, the financial return can be enormous. The value of the data to a competitor would be to save them the cost and time of the research and potentially to give them a significant advantage in bringing a product to market – again dictating the need for the organisation to protect it.

When we consider the value of data at a personal level, it frequently impinges upon an individual's privacy. For example, we would be reasonably aggrieved if our local doctor's surgery published details of our ailments and treatments.

Another aspect of value is that of reputation. An organisation that can demonstrate that it treats customers' data with respect and does not distribute it without their permission will retain its competitive advantage over one that does not. There have been numerous examples in the media of organisations that have been lax in maintaining their customers' details securely, and have suffered severe reputational damage as a result.

Criminal organisations are the most obvious choice of potential beneficiary of someone else's data. They can either make use of the data itself to undertake fraud, theft, blackmail or some form of harassment, or they can sell on the data to other criminal organisations. Almost daily there are reports in the media about organisations that have had their IT systems penetrated and data extracted. One of the most worrying of these is that of the Equifax data breach that occurred in September 2017, which affected the credit records of more than 140 million people (BBC 2017). The value of this kind of data to criminal organisations is almost limitless.

Security agencies are another possible beneficiary of an organisation's – or indeed an individual's – data, since much of their intelligence information is derived from data gathered from interception and covert means in order to build a picture of their 'persons of interest'.

In the case of data value to criminals, the organisation must take great care to ensure that the data it holds is not compromised; however, in the case of security agencies, national legislation may require organisations to cooperate with them to provide access to data (including encryption keys where applicable) in order for them to maintain the country's national security interests. This may create tension between the organisation and the government body demanding the information, as in the example of Apple refusing to decrypt the iPhone of a shooting suspect in 2016 (Dredge and Yadron 2016).

Good data governance dictates that the governing bodies of organisations that distribute data must not only take great care to protect it, but also be able to demonstrate that they are doing so.

Risks

Having examined the value of data, let's turn to the risks involved in its distribution. The organisation must ensure that its operational management have developed and implemented adequate risk management processes and procedures to ensure that data is not distributed in an inappropriate manner or to unauthorised recipients.

There are two basic components to risk: the impact or consequence of something happening, such as a data breach; and the likelihood or probability that it will happen. If either the impact or the likelihood is very low, the resulting risk will also be low; however, low risks should not be ignored, but reviewed periodically to see whether impact or likelihood has changed. The art of establishing the level of risk is referred to as risk assessment, and is covered in considerably greater detail in ISO 31000:2018 – Risk management – Principles and guidelines, and in ISO/IEC 27005:2018 – Information technology – Security techniques – Information security risk management.

While it is a matter for operational management to ensure that risks are properly managed, overall responsibility for risk management remains with the governing body of the organisation, and must begin with an approved and published risk management policy. This will set out the organisation's attitude to risk, what is deemed to be acceptable and what is not, and, at a high level, what actions must be undertaken by operational management to mitigate risks.

Threats

Threats take advantage of vulnerabilities to cause an impact. There are many kinds of threat, such as hacking, physical threats, systems and service outages, abuse of administration and access, environmental disasters, accidental damage and interception of data. Threats are very difficult to address, since many of them are completely outside the organisation's control, although good security and operational management can alleviate some of those that are within it. Despite this, organisations that distribute data should be cognisant of current threats as well as being prepared to learn about and deal with new ones.

Threats that may affect the distribution of data will include:

- the lack of availability of the data;
- incorrect, garbled or corrupted data;
- the failure of transmission of the data;
- unauthorised interception of the data in transit between the distributing organisation and the recipient;
- distribution to the wrong recipient(s);
- unauthorised onward distribution by legitimate recipients to non-legitimate recipients, which can be addressed in part by the application of security controls within the information's metadata, known as information rights management.

Impacts or consequences

Impacts or consequences come as the result of a threat being carried out. In the context of data distribution, impacts are likely to be in the form of:

- operational impacts, in which distribution (or retrieval) of data cannot be undertaken due to availability issues;

- reputational impacts, in which the organisation suffers some form of adverse reaction to an unplanned event, such as the news of a data breach;

- financial impacts, in which the organisation either loses money through loss of business or data theft, or alternatively by regulatory fines for non-compliance;

- legal impacts, which also are likely to result from data breaches in which, for example, persons or organisations that suffer harm through loss or corruption of data about them may take some form of action through the courts against the organisation responsible for the loss.

Likelihood or probability

The other component of risk is referred to as likelihood or probability. Although the terms tend to be used interchangeably, there is important distinction between the two. Likelihood is a qualitative term, providing no granularity of detail, such as 'high', 'medium' or 'low'; whereas probability is a quantitative term, signifying a reasonably precise measurement, such as 10 per cent or £1 million.

Risk assessments sometimes make use of a halfway house, referred to as semi-quantitative, in that the assessments of impact and likelihood are given numerical boundaries, for example 'high' equates to a range of values between 75 and 100 per cent, 'medium' equates to a range of values between £250,000 and £500,000.

The likelihood of a threat being carried out comes partly as the result of vulnerabilities in an organisation's data assets, which can include the hardware systems, data networks, operating systems, software applications and the data itself.

Vulnerabilities

Vulnerabilities are weaknesses inherent in all aspects of data management, including data distribution. Many are straightforward to prevent or remove, and will require steps to be taken at the operational management level. There are five key areas in which vulnerabilities can be found:

- access control, in which unauthorised consumers of the data are able to access it;

- acquisition, development and maintenance, in which the systems upon which distribution is based contain fundamental flaws, such as unpatched and untested operating systems software and applications software;

- physical and environmental issues, such as systems failures and a lack of resilience of electrical power or IT systems;

- people-related issues, for example disaffected staff who may release data without approval or lower the organisation's security settings to permit unauthorised access;

- communications and operations issues, in which IT systems and services are incorrectly configured or not proactively monitored for unauthorised access.

Controls

Vulnerabilities can be removed or reduced by the application of controls – actions that are designed to deal with specific problems, either proactively or reactively – and these in turn will reduce the level of risk. Controls can fall into one of three strategic categories:

- avoiding or terminating the risk, in which the action that creates the vulnerability is stopped, for example reversing the decision to build a key office or data centre in a known flood plain;
- risk transfer or sharing, in which the vulnerability remains, but the impact or consequence is shared between two or more parties. Insurance is the most common form of risk transfer or sharing;
- risk reduction or modification, in which the vulnerability is changed in some way.

There is a fourth option: to accept the risk when its level falls below a value set in the organisation's risk appetite, but this choice must always be taken with the understanding that threats and/or likelihood could change over time and that the level of risk could increase. Accepted risks must always be reviewed at intervals, and must never be ignored. If any of the three main options are adopted, there may also be some remaining or residual risk, which again must be acknowledged and monitored on an ongoing basis.

At the next level, the tactical level, there are four different methods of applying controls. These are:

- detective controls, which, for example, identify when unauthorised access has occurred;
- preventative controls, which stop something from happening once it has been detected;
- directive controls, such as security policies, which inform operational staff what steps must be taken before, during or after an incident has occurred;
- corrective controls, which provide the more technical level of detail required to fix a problem.

Finally, there are the operational-level controls that provide the greatest degree of granularity to operational staff:

- procedural controls, which describe in detail exactly what actions are to be taken, by whom and in which order;
- physical controls, such as door locks and closed-circuit television systems to monitor access to secure areas;
- technical controls, such as the configuration settings for key IT systems and servers.

Once controls have been implemented, it is good practice to reassess the level of risk in order to verify that the controls have been effective, and again to monitor them on an ongoing basis.

Data sensitivity and classification

Where the distribution of sensitive data is concerned, it is vital that organisations understand how to rate its sensitivity; that is, how to decide with whom it can be shared and the potential consequences of sharing it beyond the agreed or acceptable limits.

This relates back to the GDPR mentioned earlier, in that any information that the organisation holds about individuals (data subjects) must be stored, handled and distributed bearing in mind the privacy and rights of those data subjects. Failure to do so may result in penalties, such as fines based on the organisation's financial turnover.

Organisations will inevitably develop their own scheme for the classification of data, but this can be confusing, especially when sharing data between organisations who have adopted different terminology. This is especially true when exchanging data with the public sector, which operates its own security classification scheme. Whatever scheme is used, it is important that organisations define exactly what they mean by terms such as 'confidential' or 'secret', and they must take steps to inform organisations who may be in receipt of the data of how their scheme operates and how the received data must be handled.

In order to achieve this, it is worth looking briefly at a system used internationally to define what data may be shared – especially within and between organisations involved in work of a sensitive nature. The scheme (originally developed in the USA, but later refined in the UK) is known as the Traffic Light Protocol (ENISA n.d.), and defines four colours: Red, Amber, Green and White, as described below:

> **RED** information may not be shared or disclosed outside the very limited sharing circle. It is normally highly sensitive in nature, and disclosure could cause significant financial or reputational damage.

> **AMBER** information may be shared within a somewhat larger circle, but its distribution must be restricted to those with a genuine need to know. The person or organisation sharing Amber information will normally specify the limits beyond which the information may not be shared.

> **GREEN** information may be more widely disclosed within the community or communities to which it relates, but must not be made accessible to the public-at-large – for example via the open internet.

> **WHITE** information may be distributed publicly, but will normally be subject to the standard rules of copyright.

There is a further rule for the sharing of information, which is often invoked at meetings or conferences: the Chatham House Rule. This states that when meetings are held under the Rule, participants may make use of the information they learn, but they may not reveal either the identity or affiliation of speakers or of other participants (Chatham House n.d.).

Additionally, and whatever the sensitivity rating applied to data, it may be the case that the source of the data may wish to remain anonymous – often for commercial reasons. In this case, it is important for the organisation sharing the data to be able to anonymise its source as part of the overall process. A more detailed explanation of how information may be shared securely and with anonymity can be found in my paper 'Trusted information sharing for cyber security situational awareness' (Sutton 2015).

Constraints

The third area that must be considered concerns the factors constraining the distribution of data. The organisation itself should introduce policies and procedures that define precisely why and how data may be distributed or shared and to whom. It must also take into account the expectations of its intended consumers in terms of what data will be freely available, and what may be obtained solely by some form of subscription. It follows also that the consumers of the data must be informed of procedures for how the data must be handled by them, and in some cases their agreement to adhere to these may be required.

Legislation and regulation
Data protection and GDPR legislation are some of the most stringent constraints faced by organisations collecting, processing and distributing data. It is imperative that the governing body ensures that proper data protection procedures are followed and that evidence of this is retained for the purposes of audit and scrutiny.

In some instances, distributing organisations may have a contractual obligation to provide data to consumers at certain times of day. However, it should be possible (and contracts should include the facility) for the distribution mechanisms to be out of service for maintenance and upgrade purposes – a point that is frequently overlooked.

Accessibility of data
In certain cases, there may be a requirement to present the data in a form that is accessible to consumers who suffer from visual impairment. This may require the data to be formatted with a large typeface or provided audibly as well as, or instead of, pure text.

It is also important that, where possible, the data is presented in a form that does not require specialist software, so that recipients can view it without difficulty. A commonly used format is Adobe's portable document format (pdf), which only requires a freely available reader.

Transmission mechanisms
Data distribution or sharing can take place in two basic ways:

- push distribution;
- pull distribution.

In the push scenario, consumers of the data will either have subscribed or simply registered to receive the data, and will normally expect to have it delivered at pre-agreed intervals. Good data governance dictates, first, that the consumers have actually given their consent or expressed a wish to receive the data, and, second, that the consumers must have the right to unsubscribe from this at any time, for example the ability to do so is normally included as a link within an outgoing email.

In the pull scenario, consumers of the data will normally access the distributing organisation's website – either with or without prior registration or subscription – or a dedicated server on the distributing organisation's wide-area network to which the consumers have been given access permissions. Subscribed or registered consumers will expect this method of access to be available at all times within the constraints of the contract.

SUMMARY

In this chapter, we began by examining the hierarchy of data and how it relates to information and knowledge, and the basic aspects of information security – confidentiality, integrity and availability. We then moved onto the models of distributing data – the free and the subscription models.

Next, we turned to the value of data, not only the value to the distributing organisation, but also to consumers of the data and to other possible entities who might have an interest – legitimate or otherwise – in acquiring it.

Then, we examined the risks associated with data distribution; the quality and sensitivity of data being distributed or shared, based on the impacts caused by threats; and the likelihood of the risks, influenced by vulnerabilities, and the controls used to treat the risks.

Finally, we covered the constraints imposed on the distributing organisation, either by its own policies or by external influences such as legislation and regulation, accessibility and the technical mechanisms by which data is distributed.

Having read and understood these points, the governing bodies of distributing organisations should be well placed to make objective decisions regarding the process of distribution in a secure way that provides value both to the organisation itself, and to its data consumers.

10 DISPOSE

Alison Holt

We use variants of the word 'dispose' in the English language in several different ways, including the following examples:

- chilling words in a crime thriller, such as 'he disposed of the body';
- remarkably mundane words, such as 'he disposed of the banana skin in the bin';
- less everyday phrases, such as 'he disposed of his shares and property assets, including the family mansion';
- as a state of availability, such as 'I am fully at your disposal'.

The first example talks of an essentially non-reversible activity. In the second example, we have a person disposing of a banana skin, but not in a non-reversible way: the act of disposal here is just moving the problem along the chain to somebody else, who will now need to address the disposal of it — and anybody passing the bin before it is emptied can pick out the banana skin and take it for themselves. The third example is a less common use of the term dispose to mean 'distribute', generally appearing in a legal context, and the fourth example hints at giving over control through disposal.

The intention of the use of 'dispose' in the data accountability map in the 38505 standard is very much in the spirit of the first example. However, I have found a number of organisations who are disposing of their data thinking they are operating in an Example 1 environment, but in reality they are operating in one of the other three. In the case of Example 2, there are organisations who have disposed of the banana skin data that passers-by have later slipped on and held the disposing organisation accountable.

This chapter will provide some guidance in identifying the business data that should be disposed of and selecting an appropriate method for disposal. It isn't a one-off activity, but the feeling of achievement afterwards will make it worthwhile. It is recommended that this discipline is scheduled for regular reoccurrence; like all new habits, it will get easier the more times it is repeated.

WHY BOTHER?

Data storage is cheap, and disposal itself is hit and miss and fraught with potentially disastrous consequences, so why bother disposing of any data?

> This argument resonates well with me.
>
> I have plenty of storage space for clothes, and I don't get around to throwing out clothes that I no longer can or do wear. My eldest daughter told me she went through her wardrobe regularly and put everything that she thought she no longer needed or wanted into a recycle bag. She would keep the recycle bag close by for a month, so that mis-filed items could be withdrawn. Whatever was left after a month got to go to a charity shop. I tried her scheme and was impressed with the consequences. I could get up in the morning knowing that I could pick anything from the wardrobe and it would fit and look good. It saved me time and was liberating, although I did keep the recycle bag for a year before finally relinquishing it. Who knows when we might get that 1,000-year weather event or an invite to a 1990s fancy dress ball?

If we keep the data that we should face up to disposing alongside our good data, we cannot rely on the quality of our data or on the quality of the decisions that we make with that data. The longer we keep the wrong data, the harder it comes to pick it out and remove it. Even if we know good data from bad data, are all our staff aware that data picked from different sources should be handled differently? And a data breach resulting in the release of inaccurate data can be as, or more, damaging than a release of accurate data.

Taking the wardrobe example in the box above, we can sort through our data and hold the data that we think should be for disposal at arm's length while we work out whether our sorting algorithm or filtering mechanism is accurate. Keeping data that is not required is an unnecessary expense, however minor that expense is.

CANDIDATES FOR DATA DISPOSAL

We've established that there is value in regularly removing data from your system that could put you at unnecessary risk of a breach or that could obfuscate your quality data, but what data types fall into these categories? Here's a non-exhaustive list of data types for disposal consideration:

- Data that is no longer relevant. (Correct data but not currently used.)
- Data that is no longer valid. (Data that is no longer correct.)
- Data that carries PII that isn't being used. (It might be correct and relevant, but PII data is the hazardous waste of data.)
- Data that no longer meets requirements for accuracy.
- Data that no longer meets requirements for quality.
- Data that should no longer be held due to a time frame stipulated in legislation.

POLICY FOR DATA DISPOSAL

The 38505 governance of data standard recommends that

> the governing body should approve policies that allow for the disposal of data when the data is no longer valuable or can no longer be held.

Once you have considered the types of data that, theoretically, should be candidates for disposal, this is a good time to create a policy for data disposal. This policy will assign accountability to your data guardians responsible for disposal and will set clear indicators so that they can determine what should be disposed of, how and when it should be disposed, and who is responsible for the disposal process. In cases where disposal is in the hands of an external party, there needs to be a formal agreement in place to set clear expectations. The approval process for the disposal of data needs to be very straightforward.

The 38505 standard also recommends that 'the governing body should monitor data retention and disposal obligations and ensure that adequate processes have been implemented'. Writing policy is not a one-off task. Legislation changes, and the data needs of the organisation evolve. The policy needs to be regularly reviewed and adjusted to meet these needs.

IDENTIFICATION THROUGH THE REPORT ACTIVITY

Before you can determine which specific data can be disposed of, you need to have an idea of what you have. I'm not suggesting that you run a full audit on data held by your organisation, as this would be a long and thanklessly unnecessary task. Instead, I recommend that you run a spot audit on different types of data, to include:

- data used to support the back-office function (e.g. HR employment records);
- data used to support the finance function;
- data used to support your products and services;
- data used to inform your business and board decisions.

Many organisations who run a spot audit on HR data find that they are (at worst) paying dead people and (at best) have a few staff members who haven't updated their address or next of kin details. Once you have completed your spot audit, you can determine the best approach to replace or dispose of out of date information.

EXTERNAL TRIGGERS FOR DATA DISPOSAL

Besides the ongoing maintenance approach to data disposal, there are external triggers that will require data to be disposed. These include:

- right to be forgotten requests;
- supplier or customer contract terms;
- compliance with legislation.

Each external trigger (and some of these will be organisation-specific) will need a formal handling and review process. For example, the website hosting the New Zealand COVID-19 tracing application, NZ COVID Tracer, states that the digital diary entries are automatically deleted after 31 days. This public statement will be supported by a formal handling and review process.

> While you are in the disposal mindset, remember that there is legislation that requires you to retain data, and in some instances you are required to keep information that has been superseded or replaced. For example, a national standards body will keep copies of standards that have been replaced and are no longer in use because a lawsuit might require them to show the standards that were in place, for example, when a leaky house was built or a wiring system that caught fire was deployed.

PERMANENT REMOVAL

The 38505 standard recommends that

> the governing body should direct managers to implement an appropriate data disposal process that includes such controls as the secure and permanent destruction of the data.

Permanent removal of data is such a complicated and delicate topic and is best approached through a consideration of the risk of somebody discovering that they can read your deleted data, and the risk that the deleted data contains PII. For every piece of data produced, there are multiple copies made for back up and disaster recovery purposes, and these copies are splashed across different data centres, possibly different media types and possibly different countries.

If your deleted data appeared on the front page of tomorrow's newspaper, what sort of problems might ensue?

It is worth bearing in mind that, if your data is hosted on one electronic system or cloud service, it is likely to be hosted on many. There will be back up devices and disaster recovery systems carrying copies of your data. Thorough disposal should take account of all the systems and devices carrying these copies of your data.

The NIST in the US provides some excellent guidance through their website for the removal, sanitisation and disposal of data (NIST 2021). If you are seeking to permanently remove data, then I suggest that you ask your service provider for the expected status of data remanence (residual representation of digital data) once the suggested removal process has been followed.

ARCHIVING DATA

If disposing of data sounds a step too far because you can't be 100 per cent sure that you won't need that data again, then you could consider archiving it in a way that the data isn't accessible to the operational side of your organisation such that it could be accessed by anybody across the company. Be sure to set a follow-up date, though, to review whether the data is still needed and to dispose of it when you are certain it is not required. Storing data that should be disposed of carries an unnecessary expense and exposes an unnecessary risk that the data will be inadvertently accessed by staff or targeted by hackers.

Whatever you do to your data, don't forget your downstream data – the data that you have sold on or passed on to partners and other stakeholders. Depending on the contractual agreement with your partners/stakeholders, this data may or may not be retrievable once passed on.

BALANCING VALUE, RISK, CONSTRAINT

By this stage in the chapter, you are possibly wishing you could go back to the days of paper records, but paper records had their own governance issues: documents were easily destroyed by mistake or removed on purpose. And permanent paper disposal has its own challenges; take, for example, the Iranian US Embassy occupation in Tehran in 1979, when sensitive documents were pieced together from shredded paper.

With electronic records we find ourselves juggling value, risk and constraint to determine our organisational policy and practice for data disposal. Storing data that is no longer valuable is obviously not a good idea, but if you cannot distinguish between valuable and non-valuable data then you have a bigger problem, and you are not alone. The results of the spot audits will provide a clear indication of the state of your data, and these might trigger a data cleansing exercise to ensure that your business is running from accurate data. Policy and practice can assist with maintaining the new data-tidy state with clean, accurate data, and triggers can be put in place to prompt updates to data based on internal and external changes to maintain data currency.

Constraints (imposed by legislation and self-imposed) must be addressed in such a way that it is possible to prove that they have been addressed. In the NZ COVID Tracer example, supporting policy and process can assist in deleting data and triggers can ensure that data is deleted within the stated time constraint.

SUMMARY

Your data disposal regime will depend on the sensitivity of your data and your confidence that you won't need it again. If you have any doubts, there is always the option of moving your 'disposed data' to offline storage.

And, finally, if you really feel the need to hoard all your data and keep it in one big data collection, then at least add labels so that you and all your staff, contractors and partners can determine your reliable from your non-reliable data.

AFTERWORD

Alison Holt

Fifty years ago, large organisations hosted bulky computers in secure, air-conditioned, humidity-controlled buildings, set apart from the rest of the organisational campus. These computers were operated by computer technicians and engineers, who often worked in isolation with their hardware. In just a few years, these digital systems moved from specialist systems set at the edge of an organisation to systems whose functions supported the role of just about every staff member.

Similarly, over the years processing data has moved from the realm of data scientists and database experts to an everyday activity for most people. Where digital systems moved from a specialist function to a core function, data systems have moved from specialist business application processing, such as weather forecasting, to providing the most valuable business assets and timely information to meet our personal needs. For many organisations, data doesn't just guide the development of a product or service, data is the product or service.

Setting up a business today would look very different from setting up a business 20, 50 or 100 years ago. You might be part of an organisation that has been running for hundreds of years and is used to gradually adapting to new services, systems and technologies as they arise. You might be part of a young start-up that has an operational model with data services at the core. The organisation I work for has leapfrogged from providing paper-based services to state-of-the-art data-enabled digital services in a matter of a few years.

With the guidance in this book contributed by international experts from across the globe, we provide a useful reference whatever the size, sector, structure or location of your organisation. The final part of the book, Appendix A, provides an example of a common data governance issue which occurs when sector agencies and regulatory bodies each work from their own data definitions and classifications, rather than work together to define common terms.

With good data governance in place, you will be set up to build a sustainable business through maximising the value of your most precious asset: data. Better governance drives better decisions, and better decisions can only drive better outcomes.

And with that I wish you the happiest of outcomes as you soar above your competitors!

APPENDIX A
GOVERNING DATA: DEALING WITH REGULATIONS

Benoit Aubert, Nathalie de Marcellis-Warin and Abdelaziz Khadraoui

This appendix highlights the governance of data challenges relating to regulations and regulatory compliance, and suggests a way forward using ontological mapping – that is the mapping of similar concepts from one legal structure to another – to highlight weaknesses relating to data collection and use in a compliance framework. The example provided relates to the transportation of hazardous substances in Canada. Data collected to meet the requirements of the Environmental Emergency Regulations is not aligned with the data collected to meet the requirements of the Transport of Dangerous Goods Act. As such, loopholes open up that support undesirable and dangerous behaviours. Similar conflicts have occurred in banking regulation where a UK bank trading in Europe could not be simultaneously compliant with the data requirements of the UK Banking Reform Act and European banking regulations.

Good governance of data practices can assist legislators in developing regulation that doesn't conflict with existing regulation and legislation, that isn't open to misinterpretation and that doesn't deliver unintended consequences.

Governance of data covers an array of activities, from the identification and the collection of data, its storage, use and distribution, to final disposal. Data comes from a wide variety of sources, in different formats. Data is increasingly used not only to inform the conduct of activities, but also for conformity reasons. We need to report on data activities conducted to various stakeholders, notably government agencies. Organisations are subject to audits on many aspects of their activities, and they must demonstrate that they have followed laws and regulations. Therefore, one type of data that is growing rapidly in organisations is that related to regulations and regulatory compliance.

Two forces are at play in explaining increased regulations. First, governments are under pressure to regulate corporate activities, following events such as the global financial crisis of 2008/09 (Moshirian 2011) or industrial disasters (CBC 2014). Second, globalisation means that companies have to comply not only with their domestic laws and regulations, but also with the regulations of countries in which they trade. They have to ensure their subcontractors comply with specific rules in their own country and in the country in which the subcontractor is based.

This growth of data management associated with regulations and conformity activities is connected to the increased complexity of data management, and the proliferation of data sources that organisations are dealing with (Lenzerini 2011).

In order to cope with the data associated with the regulatory framework in which the organisation operates, it is very important to develop an integrated view of the regulations themselves, and of the data they require. Unfortunately, laws and regulations are produced by different government departments at different levels (federal, provincial/state, municipal) without significant coordination. They use different terminologies and classifications, they introduce different reporting requirements and, in the end, organisations have to untangle them all.

As mentioned by Khatri and Brown (2010), good data management includes the addition of metadata explaining the meaning and providing the description of the data. In regulations, there is usually a list of definitions, which could be similar to metadata. Unfortunately, each law or regulation provides a new set of definitions, not necessarily easily compatible with the other sets. Organisations have to reconcile these definitions to ensure they follow the legislator's guidelines.

One area in which laws and regulations are numerous is the transportation and storage of dangerous goods (or hazardous materials). These goods are essential to the economy, but mishandling them can have dramatic consequences (Mackrael and Robertson 2014). In addition to the regulations in place, companies establish safety practices to deal with these materials (Peignier et al. 2011). We use these regulations in this appendix to explain how ontology can facilitate data governance.

This appendix offers a way to reduce the burden associated with the diversity and multiplicity of regulations. Ontological mapping presents a visual representation that provides an easy way to see linkages between different regulations as well as the gaps and overlaps between them. This tool can help organisations deal with regulations. It can also help policy makers design better regulation. If regulation is more consistent, and if there is more coherence between different laws and regulations, it becomes easier to follow regulations and compliance increases, and, as in our example of hazardous materials, the likelihood of accidents diminishes.

To provide illustrations for ontological mapping, Canadian regulation governing the transportation of dangerous goods is used in the following discussion.

THE CHALLENGE OF DATA GOVERNANCE IN COMPLEX REGULATED ENVIRONMENTS

Industrial activity requires the production, use and transport of hazardous materials for a variety of reasons. These materials present risks on industrial sites, but also between these sites due to transportation. The legislative framework surrounding hazardous materials, new or residual, seeks to protect the health of the population, the workers and the environment.

Companies transporting hazardous materials must comply with a large number of laws and regulations from different ministries (Transportation, Environment, Health, Public Safety, etc.); it is not an easy task. Rules are not assembled nicely around each type of hazardous material. They are usually grouped by types of usage. There are rules for storage, use, road transportation, rail transportation, maritime transportation and so on, but also rules for specific substances (for instance, hydrocarbons regulation).

Understanding of all the regulations related to the storage and the transport of hazardous material is extremely challenging. An even bigger task is identifying all the information required to adopt the appropriate procedures and to comply with the regulations. By failing to comply with all components of the regulations, companies are transgressing the law and, more importantly, putting at risk their staff and the general public. It becomes paramount to provide support for integrated understanding of data in a complex regulatory environment.

Finding the relevant information pertaining to the hazardous material used is not the only challenge. Organisations are also required to keep track of the material they use, file specific reports pertaining to storage, movement and usage of these goods, and keep historical data to be able to show compliance if audited. It creates a serious data collection challenge for organisations, given the lack of integration of legal requirements.

One approach to tackle the challenge associated with the multiplicity of regulations is to formally model regulations. Modelling regulations is a way to facilitate how different legal frameworks overlap or complement each other. It can highlight areas where there are contradictions between different regulations, or where one provides stricter guidelines than another, thus making the less demanding one irrelevant. Proper modelling of regulations can:

- provide a vision of the regulatory framework as a whole;
- simplify the understanding of regulation and its implementation;
- identify clearly the data related to each regulation, along with the responsibility associated with data management;
- obtain a regulatory overview almost personalised by sector of activity.

Modelling the Canadian regulations governing the transportation of dangerous goods enables us to understand the interactions between the different levels of regulation and to have a global vision of regulatory constraints associated with the logistics activities associated with transporting hazardous materials. It also enables us to identify the inconsistencies, contradictions or gaps between each level or each regulation.

The modelling strategy used in this appendix can be used for any type of regulation where there is complexity, and multiple sources of constraints. For instance, in addition to data management and protection regulation, it could easily be used for financial regulations. Financial data and activities are subject to complex regulations, emanating from different countries (where firms are trading or do business) and from international agencies.

KEY ONTOLOGICAL CONCEPTS

This section investigates the benefits of introducing ontological modelling to improve data governance by clearing confusion and ambiguity, for example where different agencies or organisations working together are using different terms for the same item or concept.

The goal of modelling is to provide an integrated map clearly showing the relationships between different concepts. It is also a way to formalise rules that are often hidden behind language. In addition, models simplify vocabulary. By standardising the use of terms, models can highlight the fact that different sources refer to the same elements using different words. This is often a challenge when trying to manage organisational data sources.

As shown in Figure A1, an ontological mapping of the laws and regulations involve identifying all the important concepts in the regulatory environment, the management rules linking concepts together and the role associated with these.

Figure A1 Ontological modelling

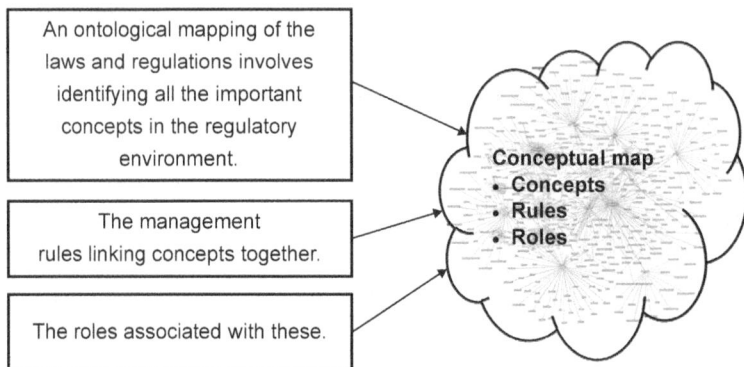

From the laws and regulations, we can extract a conceptual map. This tool enables us to express, share, discuss, build and evaluate the knowledge *described in these regulations*. It is a graphical representation of a knowledge space. It consists of concepts and semantic relationships between concepts.

Models are a representation of reality. Good ontological models enable clarity in their representation of reality. By clarity, we mean that each significant element in reality will be represented in the model (ontological completeness) and that there will be only one way to represent each element (minimising ontological overlap) (Dussart et al. 2004).

STEPS REQUIRED TO BUILD THE MAP

The sequence of steps required to build an ontological map is not complex. First, all key concepts (sometimes referred to as *classes*) have to be identified and defined. Then, these concepts are linked together, explaining how they are related. This enables us to see the interrelationships between each one.

Definitions are very important. They enable the identification of the elements to be considered, and ensure that synonyms are identified. Most laws and regulations contain a specific section defining all the concepts used. However, there is often no consistency between different Acts (which can emanate from different government departments). Carefully working out the list of key concepts may reveal that two different words are used for the same thing in two different sets of regulations.

Once the key concepts have been identified, linkages between the concepts are established. In this appendix, we will use three types of linkages: existence, instance and specialisation (see Figure A2).

Figure A2 Establishing linkages between concepts

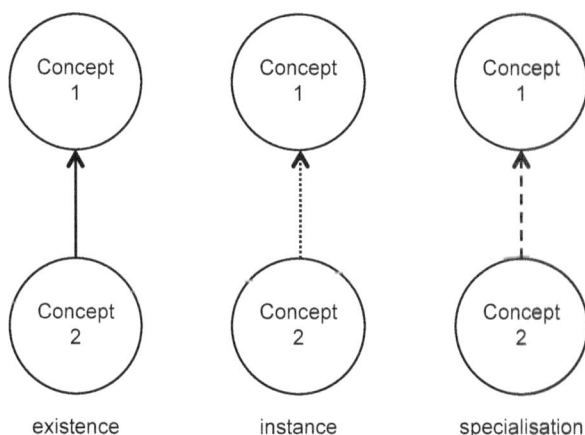

Existence is the most common type of linkage. It is represented by a regular line. If Concept 2 is linked with Concept 1 by a straight line, it means that Concept 2 cannot exist without Concept 1. For example, if we consider a car, Concept 1 could be 'dangerous product' and Concept 2 could be 'property of the product' (i.e. corrosive, flammable, explosive, etc.). The concept 'property of the product' cannot exist without the 'dangerous product' existing first.

The second type of link is the instance. It is represented by a dotted line. An instance is a specific case of a concept, normally highlighted to trigger specific actions or conditions. For example, if we refer back to our example of a 'dangerous product', gas would be an instance of a dangerous product.

Finally, the last type of relationship is the specialisation (or generalisation if the relationship is observed the other way), which is represented with a line of dashes. This means that a concept is a special case of a more general concept. For example, using again the example of the concept 'dangerous product', 'hydrogen' and 'propane' would be specialisations. The former is a generalisation of the two specialisations.

In the field of modelling information systems, maps or models are often used to understand or to represent a domain in relation to a specific information system. The use of maps (as a conceptual graph or in the form of semantic network) is not new. We can trace examples in the work of Quillian (1968) and Woods (1975). The use of ontology has expanded beyond its original usage in information systems. For example, medicine has been an area where ontologies have been developed (Rector et al. 1998).

More recently, ontology modelling has been the basis used to formalise construction safety knowledge (Zhang et al. 2015), regulatory compliance (Sadiq and Governatori 2015) and food traceability (Pizzuti et al. 2014).

USING ONTOLOGY TO IMPROVE REGULATORY DATA GOVERNANCE

This section suggests how ontology can be used to improve regulatory data governance.

Definitions

The first step to using ontology (the description of concepts and categories in a way that highlights properties and interrelationships) to improve regulatory data governance, involves the clear identification and definition of the key concepts. In our example this enables the immediate identification of challenges associated with the management of data associated with dangerous goods. We will use our simple example to illustrate this.

In the Canadian Transportation of Dangerous Goods Act, the goods are classified into nine classes according to the type of hazard they present:

1. explosives;

2. gases;

3. flammable liquids;

4. flammable solids;

5. oxidising substances and organic peroxides;

6. toxic and infectious substances;

7. radioactive materials;

8. corrosive substances;

9. miscellaneous products.

In this first categorisation, ethane is classified as a gas (class 2).

The Environment Emergency Regulation, an agency of the Government of Canada, uses a different classification for the products covered by the regulation. There are three categories:

1. substances likely to explode;

2. substances hazardous when inhaled;

3. other hazardous substances.

In this second categorisation, ethane is classified as a substance likely to explode.

Immediately, we see that for the hundreds of dangerous products classified, the definitions become key, since users of the products cannot rely on the labels used by the different regulations. Several substances labelled simply as 'gas' in one regulation are 'likely to explode' in the other. Intuitively, one would think that they could have been labelled 'explosive' in the first regulation. This is not the case.

To increase the confusion, in the environmental regulation, only the chemical components (substances) are mentioned. In the Transportation of Dangerous Goods Act, the elements specified take a variety of forms. They can be chemical components, but also products such as ammunition, bombs, detonators and so on. In this case, it then becomes very difficult to track, since on one side the end product is considered, while on the other side one would have to identify the chemical components of the product to follow the appropriate environmental procedure.

Having a dictionary with clear definitions of the concepts is a first step towards understanding the data needed to meet regulatory obligations. However, the key benefits come from the development of a conceptual map, linking the different concepts together.

IDENTIFYING THE CONCEPTS TO CREATE A MAP

When assessing the regulatory concepts, it is important to extract from the legal documents all the relevant units that have to be considered. For example, a fragment of law based on the Transportation of Dangerous Goods Act 1992[1] describes the general parameters of the law. This fragment of law presents a few conditions to be met for anyone who engages in importing, transport services, handling or the transportation of dangerous goods (see Figure A3).

From this segment of legislation, it is possible to extract key concepts of the field of activity related to the transport of dangerous goods. These concepts can be considered pivotal concepts. They are concepts considered central for the activities related to the transport of dangerous goods.

In the example presented in Figure A3, there are several pivotal concepts to extract from the Act fragment: person, import, handle, transport, dangerous goods, safety requirements, regulations, documents (accompanying), means of containment, means of transport, safety standards, safety marks.

---

1 Transportation of Dangerous Goods Act 1992, Government of Canada, current to 28 February 2017. Last amended on 1 January 2017, https://lois-laws.justice.gc.ca/PDF/T-19.01.pdf.

Figure A3 Excerpt from Transportation of Dangerous Goods Act 1992, p. 5

> **General prohibition**
>
> **5** No person shall import, offer for transport, handle or transport any dangerous goods unless
>
> **(a)** the person complies with all safety requirements and security requirements that apply under the regulations;
>
> **(b)** the goods are accompanied by all documents that are required under the regulations
>
> **(c)** a means of containment is used for the goods that is required or permitted under the regulations; and
>
> **(d)** the means of containment and means of transport comply with all safety standards that apply under the regulations and display all applicable safety marks in accordance with the regulations
>
> 1992, c.34, s. 5; 2009, c. 9, s. 4.

A partial map has been developed in Figure A4 to show how these elements are represented. The representation will be compared with other maps of associated regulations later in the appendix.

Figure A4 Transportation of Dangerous Goods map (partial view)

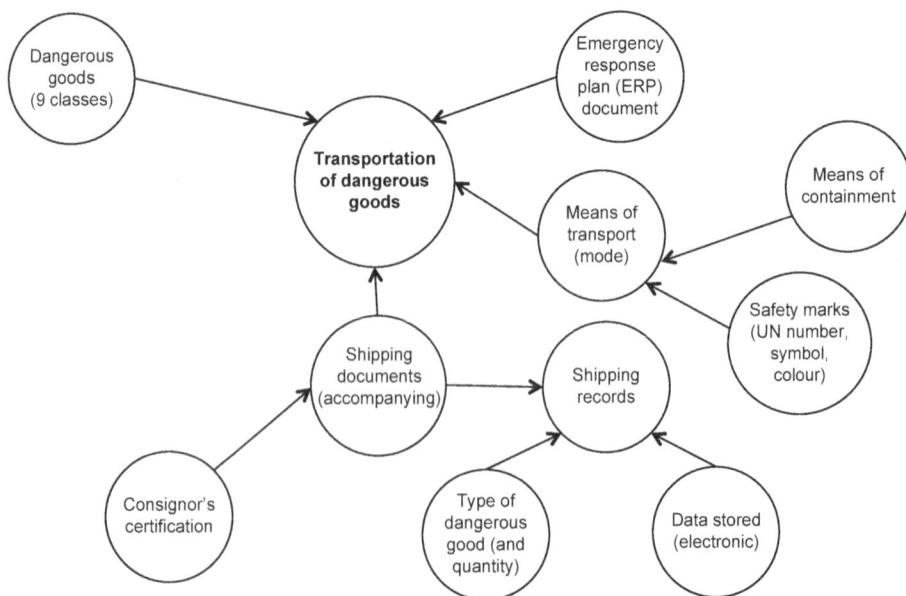

The ontological models used to describe the domain of hazardous material transportation are built around these pivotal concepts. To complement the map, we have to identify the rules and the roles associated with these concepts.

IDENTIFYING THE RULES

Rules define procedures within an institution. Rules define the constraints that govern the execution by the players of one or more activities. Rules enable the coordination of the activities among the various stakeholders, while establishing ethical rules to ensure the quality of activities. Their validation is the responsibility of actors, and controls are established to determine sanctions when necessary (Khadraoui 2007).

Consider the example of section 7.3 of the Transport of Dangerous Goods Act in Figure A5. This section of the Act sets out a rule that specifies the need to follow security training and the need for a security plan before any import activity, transport or handling of hazardous materials. This rule concerns business activities 'import a hazardous material' and 'handling of dangerous materials' and the activity 'transport of dangerous material'.

Figure A5 Excerpt from Transportation of Dangerous Goods Act 1992, p. 8

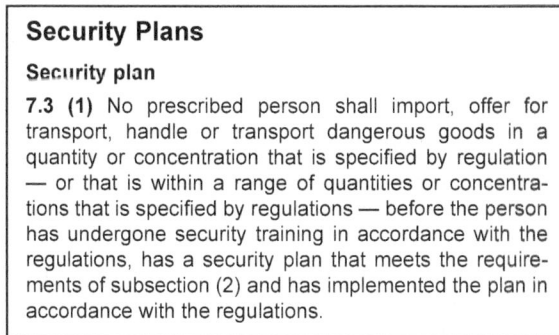

Security Plans

Security plan

7.3 (1) No prescribed person shall import, offer for transport, handle or transport dangerous goods in a quantity or concentration that is specified by regulation — or that is within a range of quantities or concentrations that is specified by regulations — before the person has undergone security training in accordance with the regulations, has a security plan that meets the requirements of subsection (2) and has implemented the plan in accordance with the regulations.

Later in the Act, the various documents and records required to be maintained are described, as well as the powers of inspectors and the types of audits that can be conducted. Finally, consequences (personal liability and financial responsibilities) if the conditions specified are breached, are described.

IDENTIFYING THE ROLES

An ontological role is a specific organisational role that is not questioned by the development of the information system or by the organisation of the data. A role defines what a participant given the role may do or may request from other participants or from systems (Zhu and Zhou 2006).

A role can be seen as tasks and responsibilities that are grouped together in an organisation (Hartson and Pyla 2012). Once a role is defined, it becomes possible to determine the required attributes, skills and know-how that a participant needs to perform the role. The role is associated with a specific position within an organisational context. It is attached with specific duties, levels of authority and responsibilities (Cichocki and Irwin 2014).

From the Transport of Dangerous Goods Act, it is possible to identify specific roles, as well as their associated properties. Numerous definitions are offered, and among them we can find:

> *inspector* means a person designated as an inspector under subsection 10(1); (*inspecteur*)

Later (p. 9) the Act defines who can appoint someone (or a group) to a role of inspector:

> Designation of inspectors
>
> 10(1) The Minister may designate persons or classes of persons whom the Minister considers qualified to act as inspectors for any of the purposes of this Act, and may revoke such a designation.

The duty (inspection) comes with powers to ask for specific information and proceed to specific verifications. This defines the area of authority of the inspector (p.11):

> Powers of inspector
>
> (2) In the course of carrying out an inspection under subsection (1), an inspector may
>
> (a) open and inspect, or request the opening and inspection of, any means of containment for which the inspector is designated, including any closures, valves, safety release devices or other appurtenances that are essential to the use of the means of containment to contain dangerous goods, if the inspector believes on reasonable grounds that it is being used to handle or transport dangerous goods or to contain dangerous goods offered for transport; ...

Every ontological space contains the information required for a role. For our example, a complete analysis of the transportation of the hazardous material allows us to establish a knowledge space that is associated with roles: person/organisation, Minister of Transport, Minister of National Defence, Inspector. Examination of the associated regulations adds several roles,[2] for instance: Director General, Director, Compliance and Response; Chief, Response Operations.

Formally understanding the roles determines who will produce, store or access specific data. This is an integral part of the data governance matrix required to ensure adequate governance (Khatri and Brown 2010).

---

2 https://www.tc.gc.ca/eng/tdg/clear-tofc-211.htm.

IDENTIFYING THE INCONSISTENCIES OR GAPS

Formally mapping each regulation enables the comparison and the integration of different regulatory frameworks. It also highlights gaps between regulations, or connections between two different sets of regulations. This can improve risk management practices.

For example, we looked at the regulations governing environmental protection. Several of these regulations concern material also included in the Transportation of Dangerous Goods Act. To illustrate connections between the two sets of regulations, we will use the excerpt set out in Figure A6.

Figure A6 Environmental Emergency Regulations (excerpt)

Identification of places

3 (1) Any person who owns or has the charge, management or control of a substance set out in column 1 of Schedule 1 that is located at a place in Canada, must submit to the Minister a notice containing the information requested in Schedule 2 for each such place in either of the following circumstances:

(a) the substance is in quantity that at any time is equal to or exceeds the quantity set out in column 3 of Schedule 1 for that substance; or

(b) the substance is in quantity that is greater than zero and is stored in a container that has maximum capacity equal to or exceeding the quantity set out in column 3 of Schedule 1 for that substance.

2 In determining quantity for the purpose of subsection (1), the person must include all quantities of the substance that are located at the place, whether in storage or in use, except the following:

(a) quantities of the substance that are temporarily stored for 72 hours or less in a container not normally located at the place, if the person keeps evidence during the temporary storage period of the date the substance was received;

The concept map shown in Figure A7 is developed from the Environmental Emergency Regulations excerpt in Figure A6. It describes what has to be reported when substances are kept. As can be seen on the map, the storage of a substance in a fixed place (duration of storage more than 72 hours) triggers the production of a notice to the government minister.

This simple statement, when combined with the regulation on transportation, shows how complete documentation of regulation could facilitate proper management of dangerous material.

Figure A7 Environmental Emergency Regulations map (partial view)

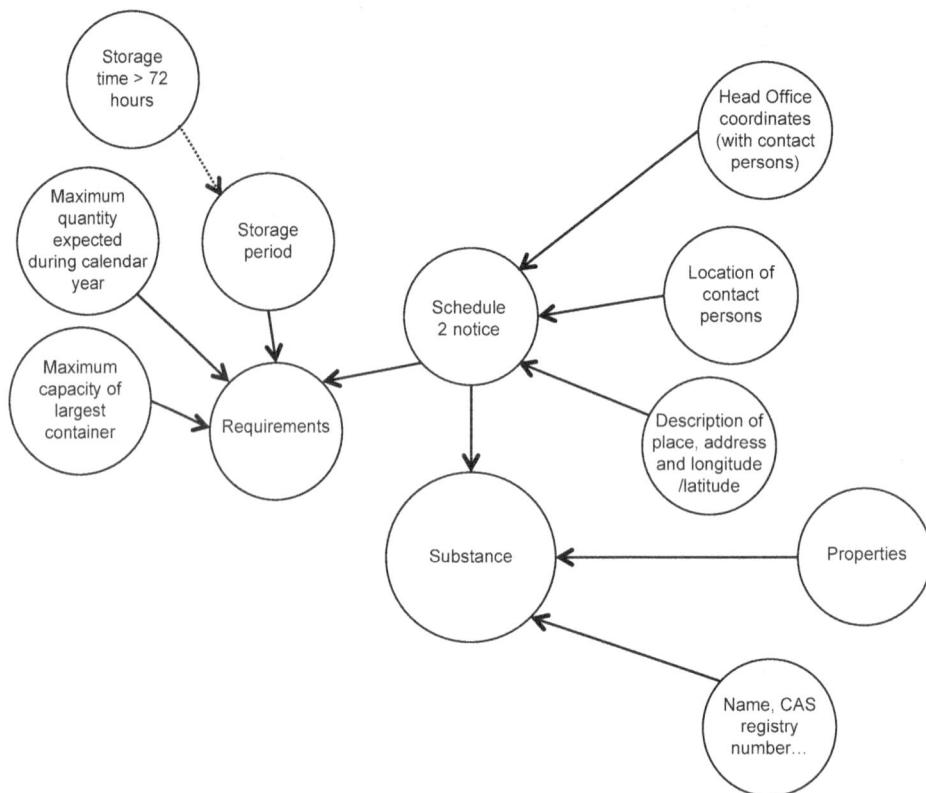

Consider the situation of a lorry stopped in a yard for more than 72 hours. Under the Environmental Emergency Regulations, the entity in charge of the transportation should provide a notice to the minister. However, by simply moving the lorry around, the containment remains under the Transportation regulations, and is not subjected to the Environment regulations. This means that for weeks the same merchandise could be moved every three days and remain out of scope of the Environment Emergency Regulations.

Clearly, this was not the intention of the legislator. Storing permanently dangerous substances in a lorry tank is not desirable, but having the same lorry circling around the town to avoid storage regulations is an even worse situation. Obviously, there is a gap between transportation and environmental protection regulatory provisions.

A clear ontological mapping of laws would formally link the two sets of regulations. It then becomes easier to see which provisions apply in which case, and we can identify the associated risks of opportunistic behaviour when one provision is not as strict as the other.

Such a global view would be useful for both the regulator and the commercial organisations. For instance, the 'shipping records' and the 'emergency response plan' specified in the Transportation of Dangerous Goods Act could be used to prevent the artificial movement of goods to avoid the 72-hour limit, and to integrate into the plan specific measures for the environmental regulations. Shipping records share data with the Schedule 2 notice. Harmonising legal documents would simplify data management and facilitate compliance.

DEVELOPMENT OF A GLOBAL VISION OF REGULATORY CONSTRAINTS

Providing a map of regulations also enables the identification of overlaps between different Acts or Regulations. For instance, when considering the section of the Transportation of Dangerous Goods Act pertaining to marine environment (sending material by ship), several other regulations have to be considered simultaneously. To illustrate this, we show in Figure A8 how modelling enables us to connect directly the regulations emanating from the International Maritime Organization (shown in the circles with dotted lines) into the model built for Canadian regulation about dangerous goods.

Figure A8 Possible addition to the map if IMDG Code is included

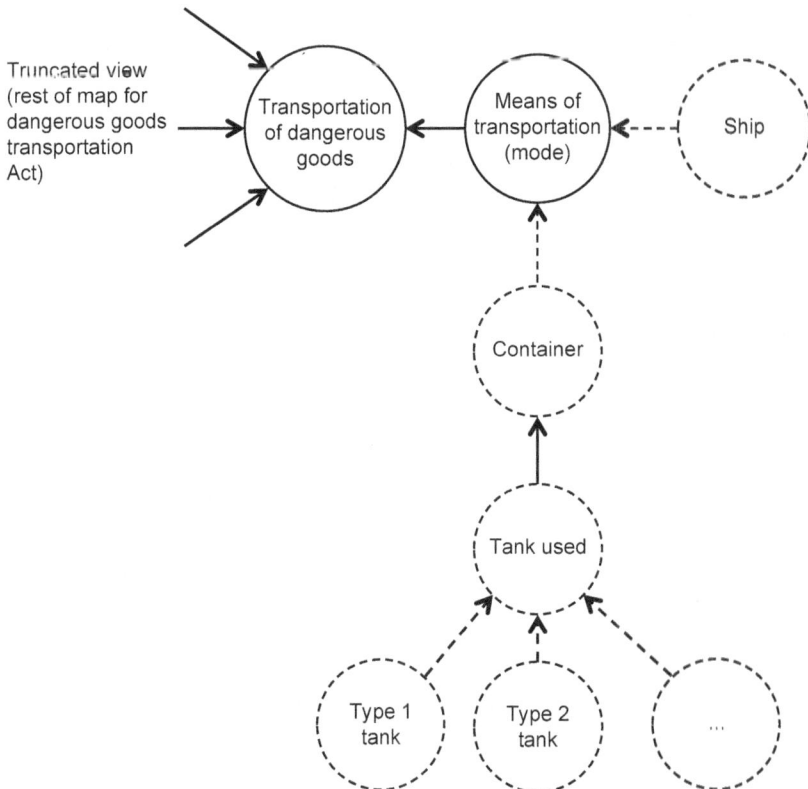

Connecting the International Maritime Dangerous Goods (IMDG) Code from the International Maritime Organization is relatively easy. When the transportation mode becomes 'Ship' and when material is included in a form of container, we have to look at the specific type of portable tank used for the material shipped. This will trigger specific guidelines (quantity that has to be in the portable tank, for example).

In order to have a comprehensive view of the regulations related to the shipment of dangerous goods by sea, it is important to take into account the information described in the law on the transport of dangerous goods and the regulations, but also to explore and analyse the Canada Shipping Act 2001,[3] the Marine Transport Security Act 1994[4] and the Safe Container Convention Act 1985.[5] Having an ontological model enables an integrated view of constraints faced by organisations.

ASSESSING THE IMPACT OF LEGISLATIVE CHANGE

Using ontological maps would also be useful to assess the impact associated with legislative change. By having a visual representation of the law, it is possible to see more easily the possible repercussions associated with probable changes to the law.

The first element to be considered is the list of definitions. If the legal change is modifying the definition, does it improve (or retain) coherence with the definitions and the classifications used in other regulations? This is not trivial. The more complex and disjointed regulations are, the less likely organisations will comply with them in their entirety. It increases the odds of errors that, in the case of dangerous goods, can be fatal.

The second element to consider is the new map. By introducing the modification, maps will be changed. All the ramifications within the current regulation would be made visible. This could be published by government agencies. It would provide a clear indication of the changes, for instance, by simply using a colour scheme that would highlight areas where organisations may have to modify their approach, the data they collect or the allocation of responsibilities related to the new regulation.

MOVING FORWARD

Governance of data is a complex activity for an organisation. Governance of data associated with regulations is even more complex. It requires the constant monitoring of laws domestically and internationally and requires practice to be continually adjusted to reflect regulatory change. In addition, there is a requirement to keep data such that the organisation can demonstrate conformity.

One approach suggested to address the management of regulatory data is the use of ontological modelling. This facilitates the identification of relevant regulations and

---

3   https://laws-lois.justice.gc.ca/eng/acts/c-10.15/.

4   https://www.tc.gc.ca/eng/acts-regulations/acts-1994c40.htm.

5   https://laws-lois.justice.gc.ca/eng/acts/S-1/.

enables managers to see how different regulations are tied together. When available, ontological maps also provide support for lawmakers to devise better integrated regulatory environments.

Where we have multiple agencies providing overlapping functions and services, and where those agencies develop their own data terms, role responsibilities and systems independently of each other, we introduce confusion and loopholes for those who look to the agencies for guidance or who are bound to be compliant with agency guidance. Good data governance practice involves mapping these terms so that responsibilities can be understood by all stakeholders.

This appendix offers examples to illustrate how such maps can help to identify gaps, overlaps and connections between different regulations. Once these issues with the regulatory environment are identified, conformity is easier to achieve.

Building an ontological map for regulation is not an easy task. It is akin to developing an integrated set of metadata for regulations in a given domain. For the transportation of dangerous goods described in this appendix, it would mean integrating several laws within the same country, in addition to numerous international regulations.

While it is unlikely that an organisation would undertake this task by itself, it is possible to envision partial automation in the generation of models, as well as a crowdsourcing approach (Getman and Karasiuk 2014). This would enable the creation of the models *and* their maintenance. A crowdsourcing approach would also increase public awareness of these regulations. For domains such as dangerous goods, this would be a desirable consequence.

REFERENCES

ABC.net.au (2019) Ardern lashes Facebook over failing to stop spread of Christchurch shooter's live stream. *ABC News*. https://www.abc.net.au/news/2019-03-19/new-zealand-facebook-christchurch-shooting-video-sheryl-sandberg/10915184.

Auto-ISAC (2016) Best practices executive summary. https://automotiveisac.com/best-practices/.

BBC (2017) Massive Equifax data breach hits 143 million. *BBC News*, 7 September. https://www.bbc.co.uk/news/business-41192163.

CAA (2021) *The Drone and Model Aircraft Code*. UK Civil Aviation Authority. https://register-drones.caa.co.uk/drone-code.

CBC (2014) Lac-Mégantic: Lisa Raitt announces rail safety rules based on crash findings. *CBC News*, 29 October. https://www.cbc.ca/news/politics/lac-m%C3%A9gantic-lisa-raitt-announces-rail-safety-rules-based-on-crash-findings-1.2816680.

Chatham House (n.d.) Chatham House Rule: The Chatham House Rule is used around the world to encourage inclusive and open dialogue in meetings. Chatham House. https://www.chathamhouse.org/about-us/chatham-house-rule.

Cheney, D., Reiner, J. and Cheney, L. (2014) *Heart: An American Medical Odyssey*. Thorndike.

Cichocki, P. and Irwin, C. (2014) *Organization Design: A Guide to Building Effective Organizations*, 2nd edn. Kogan Page.

DCMS (2018a) Code of practice for consumer IoT security. Department for Digital, Culture, Media & Sport. https://assets.publishing.service.gov.uk/government/uploads/system/uploads/attachment_data/file/773867/Code_of_Practice_for_Consumer_IoT_Security_October_2018.pdf.

DCMS (2018b) Mapping of IoT security recommendations, guidance and standards to the UK's code of practice for consumer IoT security. Department for Digital, Culture, Media & Sport. https://assets.publishing.service.gov.uk/government/uploads/system/uploads/attachment_data/file/774438/Mapping_of_IoT__Security_Recommendations_Guidance_and_Standards_to_CoP_Oct_2018.pdf.

Dredge, S. and Yadron, D. (2016) Apple challenges 'chilling' demand to decrypt San Bernardino shooter's iPhone. *The Guardian*, 17 February. https://www.theguardian.com/technology/2016/feb/17/apple-challenges-chilling-demand-decrypt-san-bernadino-iphone.

Dussart, A., Aubert, B.A. and Patry, M. (2004) An evaluation of inter-organizational workflow modelling formalisms. *Journal of Database Management*, 15 (2), 74–104.

ENISA (n.d.) Considerations on the Traffic Light Protocol. European Union Agency for Cybersecurity. https://www.enisa.europa.eu/topics/csirts-in-europe/glossary/considerations-on-the-traffic-light-protocol.

ETSI (2019) CYBER: Cyber security for consumer Internet of Things. ETSI TS 103 645 v1.1.1 (2019-02), DTS/CYBER-0039. ETSI. https://www.etsi.org/deliver/etsi_ts/103600_103699/103645/01.01.01_60/ts_103645v010101p.pdf.

FDA (2014) Content of premarket submissions for management of cybersecurity in medical devices. US Food and Drug Administration. https://www.fda.gov/downloads/MedicalDevices/DeviceRegulationandGuidance/GuidanceDocuments/UCM356190.pdf.

FDA (2016a) Public workshop – moving forward: Collaborative approaches to medical device cybersecurity, January 20–21, 2016. US Food and Drug Administration. https://wayback.archive-it.org/7993/20171114200842/https://www.fda.gov/MedicalDevices/NewsEvents/WorkshopsConferences/ucm474752.htm.

FDA (2016b) Postmarket management of cybersecurity in medical devices: Guidance for industry and food and drug administration staff. US Food and Drug Administration. https://www.fda.gov/downloads/MedicalDevices/DeviceRegulationandGuidance/GuidanceDocuments/UCM482022.pdf.

Fenner, J. (2013) Dick Cheney feared 'Homeland' style assassination using cardioverter defibrillator. *Liberty Voice*, 19 October. https://guardianlv.com/2013/10/dick-cheney-feared-homeland-style-assassination-video/.

Fiveash, K. (2013) Royston cops' ANPR 'ring of steel' BREAKS LAW, snarls watchdog: 24-hour spycam surveillance of sleepy town deemed 'excessive'. *The Register*, 24 July. https://www.theregister.com/2013/07/24/ico_attacks_royston_ring_of_steel/.

FTC (2013) Path social networking app settles FTC charges it deceived consumers and improperly collected personal information from users' mobile address books. US Federal Trade Commission. https://www.ftc.gov/news-events/press-releases/2013/02/path-social-networking-app-settles-ftc-charges-it-deceived.

FTC (2014a) TRENDnet, Inc., in the matter of. US Federal Trade Commission. https://www.ftc.gov/enforcement/cases-proceedings/122-3090/trendnet-inc-matter.

FTC (2014b) FTC approves final order settling charges against TRENDnet, Inc. US Federal Trade Commission. https://www.ftc.gov/news-events/press-releases/2014/02/ftc-approves-final-order-settling-charges-against-trendnet-inc.

Gertz, B. (2015) NSA details Chinese cyber theft of F-35, military secrets. *The Washington Free Beacon*, 22 January. https://freebeacon.com/national-security/nsa-details-chinese-cyber-theft-of-f-35-military-secrets/.

Getman, A.P. and Karasiuk, V.V. (2014) A crowdsourcing approach to building a legal ontology from text. *Artificial Intelligence and Law*, 22 (3), 313–335.

Glass, D. (2016) Investigation into the transparency of local government decision making. Victorian Ombudsman. https://assets.ombudsman.vic.gov.au/assets/Reports/Parliamentary-Reports/1-PDF-Report-Files/Investigation-into-the-transparency-of-local-government-decision-making.pdf?mtime=20191218113407.

Greenberg, A. (2015) Hackers remotely kill a Jeep on the highway—with me in it. *Wired*. https://www.wired.com/2015/07/hackers-remotely-kill-jeep-highway/.

Hartson, R. and Pyla, P.S. (2012) *The UX Book: Process and Guidelines for Ensuring a Quality User Experience*. Elsevier.

HP (2014) HP study revealed 70 per cent of IoT devices were vulnerable to attack: IoT devices averaged 25 vulnerabilities per product, indicating expanding attack surface for adversaries. *HP News Advisory*, 29 July. https://www8.hp.com/us/en/hp-news/press-release.html?id=1744676&jumpid=reg_r1002_usen_c-001_title_r0001#.V-8R3Yh9601.

I Am The Cavalry (2016) Hippocratic oath for connected medical devices, draft. https://www.iamthecavalry.org/wp-content/uploads/2016/01/Hippocratic-oath-press-release.pdf.

Insights Team (2019) Rethinking the role of chief data officer. *Forbes*, 22 May. https://www.forbes.com/sites/insights-intelai/2019/05/22/rethinking-the-role-of-chief-data-officer/#694a42e51bf9.

Khadraoui, A. (2007) Composants de méthode pour l'ingénierie des systèmes d'information institutionnels (Doctoral dissertation, University of Geneva).

Khatri, V. and Brown, C.V. (2010) Designing data governance. *Communications of the ACM*, 53 (1), 148–152.

Lenzerini, M. (2011) Ontology-based data management. *Proceedings of the 20th ACM International Conference on Information and Knowledge Management*, 5–6.

Leyden, J. (2012) TRENDnet home security camera flaw exposes thousands: Just when you thought you were alone in the bath. *The Register*. https://www.theregister.co.uk/2012/02/07/home_video_camera_security_snafu/.

Leyden, J. (2014) Five totally believable things car makers must do to thwart hackers: Read the open letter from security pressure group. *The Register*. https://www.theregister.com/2014/08/14/car_security_manifesto/.

Mackrael, K. and Robertson, G. (2014) Lax safety practices blamed for Lac-Mégantic tragedy. *The Globe and Mail*, 19 August.

Mayo Clinic Staff (2019) Teens and social media use: What's the impact? Mayo Clinic. https://www.mayoclinic.org/healthy-lifestyle/tween-and-teen-health/in-depth/teens-and-social-media-use/art-20474437#:~:text=Social%20media%20harms&text=A%20 2019%20study%20of%20more,risk%20for%20mental%20health%20problems.

Meng-Yee, C. (2016) Great escape: How a murderer almost got away. *nzherald.co.nz*, 23 July. https://www.nzherald.co.nz/nz/news/article.cfm?c_id=1&objectid=11679757.

Miller, C. and Valasek, C. (n.d.) A survey of remote automotive attack surfaces. *Scribd*. https://www.scribd.com/doc/236073361/Survey-of-Remote-Attack-Surfaces.

Moshirian, F. (2011) The global financial crisis and the evolution of markets, institutions and regulation. *Journal of Banking & Finance*, 35 (3), 502–511.

NIST (2021) Guidelines for media sanitization. https://www.nist.gov/fusion-search?s=data+disposal.

Pane, C.E.R. (n.d.) IBM Data Center Operational; efficiency: Best practices to plan and design a data center for the 21st century. IBM LA Site and Facilities Center of Excellence. ftp://ftp.software.ibm.com/la/documents/imc/la/uy/networking/1-Carlos_Pane_IBM-Data_Center_Best_Practices-IBM_CIO_Study_Highlights-NW13.pdf.

Peignier, I., Leroux, M.-H., de Marcellis-Warin, N. and Trépanier, M. (2011) Organizational safety practices of hazardous materials carriers. *Transportation Letters*, 3, 149–159. https://doi.org/10.3328/TL.2011.03.03.149-159.

Pizzuti, T., Mirabelli, G., Sanz-Bobi, M.A. and Goméz-Gonzaléz, F. (2014) Food track & trace ontology for helping the food traceability control. *Journal of Food Engineering*, 120, 17–30.

Quillian, M.R. (1968) Semantic memory. In Minsky, M. (ed), *Semantic Information Processing*. MIT Press.

Rector, A.L., Zanstra, P.E., Solomon, W.D., Rogers, J.E., Baud, R., Ceusters, W., Claassen, W., Kirby, J., Rodrigues, J.M., Rossi Mori, A., van der Haring, E.J. and Wagner, J. (1998) Reconciling users' needs and formal requirements: issues in developing a reusable ontology for medicine. *IEEE Transactions on Information Technology in BioMedicine*, 2 (4), 229–242.

Roberts, P. (2014) Dan Geer's other keynote: Embedded devices need time to die. *the security ledger*, 4 August. Box Jump. https://securityledger.com/2014/08/dan-geers-other-keynote-embedded-devices-need-a-time-to-die/.

Sadiq, S. and Governatori, G. (2015) Managing regulatory compliance in business processes. In vom Brocke, J. and Rosemann, M. (eds), *Handbook on Business Process Management 2*. Springer.

Stats.govt.nz (2019) Quick guide to the 2018 census (updated 16 September 2019). Stats NZ. https://www.stats.govt.nz/news/quick-guide-to-the-2018-census.

Sutton, D. (2015) Trusted information sharing for cyber security situational awareness. *Elektrotechnik und Informationstechnik*, 132 (2), 113–116. https://doi.org/10.1007/s00502-015-0288-3.

UL (2017) FDA recognizes UL 2900-1 cybersecurity standard for medical devices. Underwriters Laboratories. https://www.ul.com/news/fda-recognizes-ul-2900-1-cybersecurity-standard-medical-devices.

UL (n.d.) Presenting the standard for safety for the evaluation of autonomous vehicles and other products. Underwriters Laboratories. https://ul.org/UL4600.

Wadhwa, T. and Wadhwa, V. (2012) Yes, you can hack a pacemaker (And other medical devices too). *Forbes*, 6 December. https://www.forbes.com/sites/singularity/2012/12/06/yes-you-can-hack-a-pacemaker-and-other-medical-devices-too/.

Woods, W.A. (1975) What's in a link: Foundations for semantic networks. In Bobrow, D. and Collins, A. (eds), *Representation and Understanding*. Morgan Kaufmann.

Zhang, S., Boukamp, F. and Teizer, J. (2015) Ontology-based semantic modeling of construction safety knowledge: Towards automated safety planning for job hazard analysis (JHA). *Automation in Construction*, 52, 29–41.

Zhu, H. and Zhou, M. (2006) Role-based collaboration and its kernel mechanisms. *IEEE Transactions on Systems, Man, and Cybernetics, Part C (Applications and Reviews)*, 36 (4), 578–589.

GLOSSARY

Data refers to the streams of 0s and 1s that when decoded convey **information** in the form of words, letters and numbers. Data is the term used to refer to the Information contained within an electronic filing cabinet, or **database**.

Big Data is a term used in this book for large volumes of data that cannot be handled through normal means.

The terms **digital systems** and **data systems** are used interchangeably in the media. For the purposes of this book, the term **digital systems** is used to describe the hardware or infrastructure-related context for storing data and information and **data systems** is used for a content-related context.

A **digital strategy** provides the design principles that drive the design of **digital systems** for an organisation, and a **data strategy** provides the guiding principles for the use of data within an organisation.

The terms **data products** and **data services** are used to describe data-enabled products and services provided by an organisation to internal users or external customers.

The **chief data officer** has responsibility for 'all things data' within an organisation and would be expected to create the **data strategy** for the use of data.

The **data manager** has a hands-on relationship with the data he or she manages, and a responsibility to ensure that **data quality** and other characteristics of their organisational data are fit for purpose.

Data management tasks include putting in place the tools, frameworks, storage facilities, policies, practices, systems and so on to ensure that organisational data is accessible and available in line with organisational requirements.

Data owners are owners of subsets of organisational data, and they have a key role in driving data management requirements.

Data stewards have a role that is focused on championing the use of data within an organisation and protecting against unauthorised use. They might be expected to contribute towards organisation policy and training relating to data use.

Governing body is a generic term used in this book to describe a board of directors or trustees, a cabinet committee or any other top-level group charged with setting policy rules for how their organisations use data for decision making, reference and analysis.

INDEX

NIST (US National Institute of Standards and Technology) 32, 80, 89, 100

ontological
concepts 105–6
mapping 103, 104, 106, 107, 109, 113, 114, 116, 117
modelling 105, *106*, 111, 116
roles 111–12
ontology 108
OWASP (Open Web Application Security Project) 36

PDCA (Plan Do Check Act) 16, 17, 69–70, 86
PIA (privacy impact assessment) 74
PII (personally identifiable information) 4, 7, 98, 100

principles of governance (ISO/IEC 38500) 46–52
   acquisition 48–9
   conformance 50–1
   human behaviour 51–2
   performance 49–50
   responsibility 47
   strategy 47–8
pull distribution 95–6
push distribution 95

regulation 12, 13, **23**, **25**, 30, 43, 48, 95, 96, 103–5, *111*, 113, 117
report activity 53, 99
   right to be forgotten **58**, 99
'right' data 1
risk 7, 11, 14, 19, **19–20**, 22, **23–5**, 42–3, 49, 53, 74, 80–1, 91–4
   analysis 72, 74, 78

assessment 49, 91, 92
management 43, 47, 74, 89, 91, 116
organisational 12, 18
privacy 5
probability 92

SLA (service level agreement) 62
social media 12
specialisation linkage 107

three considerations of governance (value, risk, constraint) **20**, 22, 28, 39, 41, 46, 49, 53, 64, 65, 66, 101
   Traffic Light Protocol 94

value **19–20**, 41–2, 49, 53, 79–80, 89–91